History of China

An Enthralling Journey Through Ancient Dynasties, Cultural Splendor, Revolution, and Modernization

© Copyright 2025 - All rights reserved.

The content contained within this book may not be reproduced, duplicated, or transmitted without direct written permission from the author or the publisher.

Under no circumstances will any blame or legal responsibility be held against the publisher, or author, for any damages, reparation, or monetary loss due to the information contained within this book, either directly or indirectly.

Legal Notice:

This book is copyright protected. It is only for personal use. You cannot amend, distribute, sell, use, quote, or paraphrase any part, or the content within this book, without the consent of the author or publisher.

Disclaimer Notice:

Please note the information contained within this document is for educational and entertainment purposes only. All effort has been executed to present accurate, up-to-date, reliable, and complete information. No warranties of any kind are declared or implied. Readers acknowledge that the author is not engaging in the rendering of legal, financial, medical, or professional advice. The content within this book has been derived from various sources. Please consult a licensed professional before attempting any techniques outlined in this book.

By reading this document, the reader agrees that under no circumstances is the author responsible for any losses, direct or indirect, that are incurred as a result of the use of the information contained within this document, including, but not limited to, errors, omissions, or inaccuracies.

Free limited time bonus

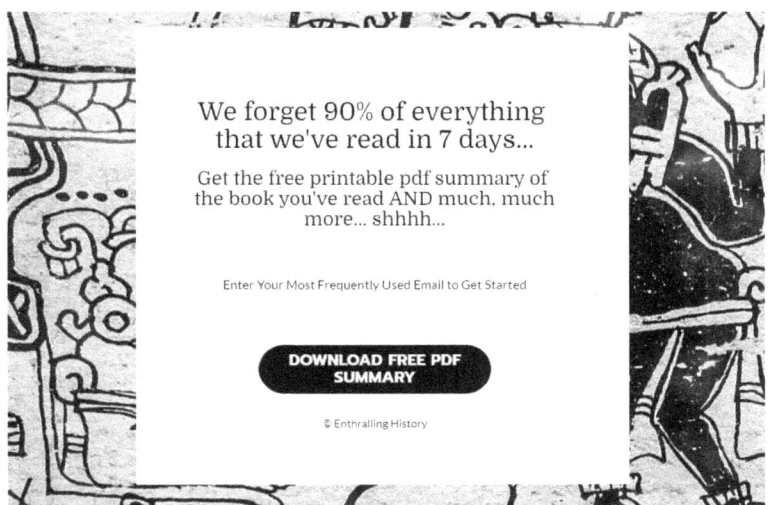

Stop for a moment. We have a free bonus set up for you. The problem is this: we forget 90% of everything that we read after 7 days. Crazy fact, right? Here's the solution: we've created a printable, 1-page pdf summary for this book that you're reading now. All you have to do to get your free pdf summary is to go to the following website:

https://livetolearn.lpages.co/enthrallinghistory/

Or, Scan the QR code!

Once you do, it will be intuitive. Enjoy, and thank you!

Table of Contents

INTRODUCTION 1
CHAPTER 1: THE PREHISTORY OF CHINA 3
CHAPTER 2: DAWN OF THE DYNASTIES 7
CHAPTER 3: SILK AND THE SWORD 16
CHAPTER 4: FROM THE TANG TO THE SONG 24
CHAPTER 5: THE MAJESTY OF THE MING DYNASTY 36
CHAPTER 6: THE QING—CHINA'S LAST DYNASTY............................44
CHAPTER 7: WORLD WAR II AND CHINA'S CIVIL WAR 62
CHAPTER 8: RED CHINA RISING 68
CHAPTER 9: A STRANGE MIX OF REPRESSION AND REFORM 77
CHAPTER 10: CHINA DURING THE 21ST CENTURY............................84
CONCLUSION: CHINA—AN EXERCISE IN STRATEGIC PATIENCE........92
FREE LIMITED TIME BONUS..94
HERE'S ANOTHER BOOK BY ENTHRALLING HISTORY THAT YOU MIGHT LIKE...95
FURTHER READING AND REFERENCE..96
IMAGE SOURCES 97

Introduction

China has a long and fascinating history. This is perhaps an understatement, considering the fact that China has been part of history since practically the beginning of the written record. As much as China is a big part of our lives today (just think of the wide range of products from Amazon or retail stores that more than likely carry the tag "Made in China"), China was also a big part of the ancient world.

The ancient Greeks knew about China, as did the Romans. China's famed Silk Road cut a path across the continent, stretching from Asia all the way to the heart of the Roman Empire. These crossroads between East and West brought not just exotic goods but also diverse cultures, innovative ideas, and even religious and philosophical expressions. The religious teachings of Buddhism and the philosophical musings of Confucianism were allowed to travel far and wide due to the routes along the Silk Road.

Westerners speak of the Golden Rule of treating others as one would like to be treated, but Confucianism has the Silver Rule, which speaks of not imposing oneself on others, just as one would not wish to be imposed upon. Even if far-flung nations did not become Confucian, it is likely that the core teachings and values of Eastern religious and philosophical systems left a lasting impression on those who heard of them.

For a long time, China seemed to be a far-off marvel. It was known to be a great and majestic civilization, but it was seemingly cut off from the rest of the world. Nevertheless, it was still at the heart of all that was valuable and worthwhile. Traders and explorers such as Marco Polo would risk life and limb just to see it with their own eyes. Outside forces gazed greedily at the riches that China had to offer, wishing to seize them for their own. It was for precisely this reason that China erected thick and sturdy walls to protect itself from the threat of incursions.

These walls could not keep everyone out, though. China would be periodically infringed upon by the Mongols, Manchus, Japanese, and Europeans. Even so, China's robust culture always proved too well entrenched for any outside force to dominate. The best they could do was temporarily oversee China's massive civilization; there was no way that they could fully control it forever. After all, China has blazed its own unique and vital path through history and will likely continue to do so for the foreseeable future.

Chapter 1: The Prehistory of China

"Death and life have their determined appointments; riches and honors depend upon heaven."

-Confucius[1]

According to tradition, China's origins date back some five thousand years; needless to say, China has a rather in-depth history, to say the least. The Chinese civilization is one of the oldest continuous civilizations on the planet. Of course, the Chinese civilization has undergone some rather incredible transformations over the millennia. Even so, there is a core group of shared ideals that has remained among the Chinese to this very day. Chinese principles regarding war, work ethic, and family life, which date back to the likes of Chinese philosophers such as Confucius, have had a strong line of continuity.

When it came to war, the Chinese believed that brains were better than brawn. Rather than rushing into battle, they preferred to outthink their enemies and figure out how to win without even fighting, if possible. That idea goes all the way back to Sun Tzu, a Chinese general and military strategist who basically said that the best kind of victory is the one you don't even have to fight for. As for work ethic, the Chinese put a huge emphasis on hard work and doing your part. Thanks to thinkers

---

[1] Brewer, D. *Quotes of Confucius and Their Interpretations: A Words of Wisdom Collection Book.* 2020. Pg. 42.

like Confucius, there was a strong sense that everyone had a role to play—whether in the family or in society—and that meant showing up, working hard, and keeping things running smoothly.

While the actual founding of China is shrouded in mystery, it is believed to date back thousands of years. Human habitation of the region goes back much further than that, at least a million years ago. This was long before recorded history and long before human civilization was even a conscious thought.

These early humans were not *Homo sapiens*, like we are today, but rather an earlier branch of humanity known as *Homo erectus*. These early humans lived in the region we now call China during the Paleolithic period. They left artifacts all across the region until they eventually disappeared from the fossil record. The exact nature of their disappearance is still the subject of some debate. Some even argue that they might not have disappeared at all; they might have merged with the newly arriving *Homo sapiens*.

Homo sapiens first appeared in the fossil record of China around 100,000 years ago. Fossilized teeth were found inside Fuyan Cave, located in modern-day Dao County in China's Hunan province. Over thousands of years, people slowly began to spread out, adapting to their surroundings and developing new ways to survive. Over time, small groups of hunter-gatherers started figuring

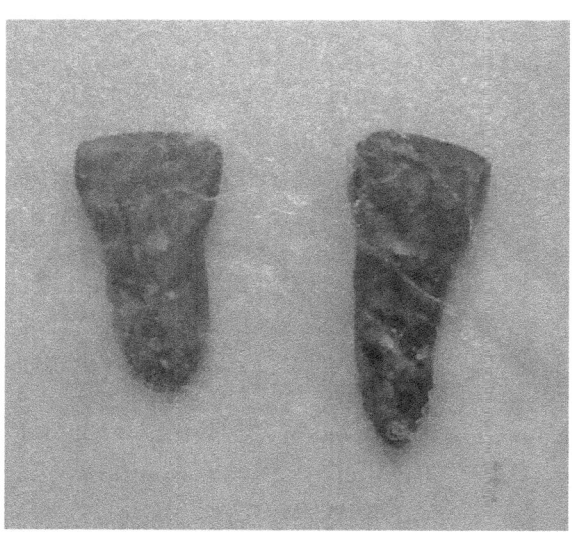

Casts of teeth of the Yuanmou Man, a subspecies of Homo erectus.[1]

out how to make better tools, build simple shelters, and maybe even form the beginnings of spoken language. It was not exactly civilization yet, but they were laying the groundwork.

During the Neolithic period, early humans first began to really band together, further building the foundation of what could be called a complex society. Instead of wandering around to forage and hunt, these early humans began to create early settlements. By doing so, they began to create the bonds of interconnectedness upon which civilization is built.

This was also the period in which widespread agriculture began to take shape. Agriculture is a key building block of any civilization. The one agricultural crop that came to dominate Chinese society was rice. Rice farms in China date back between eight thousand and nine thousand years ago. They were largely centered around China's Yangtze River. By 7000 BCE, humans lived up and down that river. By 5000 BCE, further habitation appeared along the nearby Huang He or, as it is often referred to, the Yellow River.

One group in particular, which archaeologists refer to as the Yangshao culture, took root in the Huang He Valley. This group expanded and became quite numerous. They lived near the Hung He and in the vicinity of another nearby waterway, the Wei River. The Yangshao were farmers who not only grew millet but also domesticated animals such as pigs and dogs.

Archaeologists first took note of the Yangshao culture because of their extensive pottery. They left traces of their complex pottery, which was made out of flint and jade, along the rivers where they worked and lived. They also forged complex burial sites. They dug earthen pit tombs, where they placed pottery and other important artifacts with their dearly departed. These actions seemed to indicate some early notion of an afterlife; it was as if the Yangshao were attempting to provide items that would be useful during their loved one's journey to the other side.

A pottery bottle from the Yangshao culture.[2]

Early prehistoric peoples, like the Yangshao culture, were the first to dream about the bigger things in life. They began to question who they were and where they came from. They questioned what it was that made them a unique, thinking individual, as well as what they desired from a larger society built on mutual interests. These early forays into the human condition and how it relates to the larger world would lead to the establishment of China's first major civilization.

Chapter 2: Dawn of the Dynasties

"It is better to light one small candle than to curse the darkness."
-Confucius[2]

Around 2070 BCE, the first Chinese dynasty—the Xia dynasty—was said to have emerged. For a long time, many scholars thought the Xia might have been more legend than fact. Later Chinese writers might have dreamed it up as a golden age, a shining example of what was lost when rulers got too comfortable on the throne. Like Atlantis, the Xia became a mix of memory and myth. It was part history, part cautionary tale.

But that story started to shift in the 20th century when a team of Chinese archaeologists uncovered the remains of what's now called the Erlitou culture. The site, located in Henan province, dates back to roughly the same time as the Xia dynasty is said to have existed. At first, the ruins were thought to belong to the later Shang dynasty. But over time, some researchers began linking Erlitou more closely with the Xia. Some even believe that the Erlitou site itself might have been one of the Xia capitals.

Still, not everyone agrees. Some scholars argue that the Erlitou culture had nothing to do with the Xia at all. Others go further back and trace its roots to the earlier Yangshao culture. The big challenge is that while Erlitou left behind clear archaeological remains, such as tools,

---

[2] Brewer, D. *Quotes of Confucius and Their Interpretations: A Words of Wisdom Collection Book.* Pg. 32.

pottery, weapons, and even some rather intricate bronze vessels, the Xia left no writing. Much of what we "know" about the Xia comes from texts written centuries later.

A decorative plaque from the Erlitou culture.⁸

That's part of the mystery. Among the Erlitou artifacts are basic tools like arrowheads and fishhooks, the kind you might expect from a simpler society. But mixed in are finely crafted bronze tripod containers, which are thought to have been used in ceremonies. These signs of organization and craftsmanship suggest that Erlitou might have been more than just a cluster of villages. It might have been a state-level society, with rulers, rituals, and a system for getting things done.

So, while the Xia dynasty remains shrouded in legend, Erlitou is real. Whether Erlitou was the Xia, came after it, or had nothing to do with it at all is still up for debate. But just like the ruins of Troy, what was once dismissed as pure myth is starting to look a little more like history.

Most of the information about the Xia dynasty comes from ancient chroniclers. One such chronicler, a Chinese historian named Sima Qian, who lived from around 145 to 86 BCE, recorded some vague details on the subject. He spoke of a powerful leader named Huangdi, who is better known as the Yellow Emperor. Huangdi established a powerful civilization, which, according to Sima Qian, was the direct forerunner to the Xia dynasty. Huangdi was later succeeded by his grandson Zhuanxu, who was instrumental in laying the groundwork for the Xia dynasty.

Zhuanxu was the grandfather of the man who was traditionally ascribed as the founder of the Xia dynasty, Yu the Great. Yu is a fascinating, semi-mythical figure from China's past. One of the most interesting things about him and this time period was that he led China through a terrible natural disaster, which was described as a great flood. This flood story, like many others around the world, is uncannily similar to the famous biblical account of Noah's flood.

The fact that so many parts of the world have their own ancient account of a flood from around the same time period has led many to believe that a major deluge did indeed happen. Yu the Great was instrumental in leading his people through the crisis. In fact, it is said that he found ways to literally push back against or control the rising tide, which he did through supernatural means or by way of supernatural entities. However he did it, it is said that once the floods had been pushed back, Yu was able to rebuild his kingdom and make it even better than before.[3]

Several rulers are said to have followed this founding figure, with the last one being the tyrannical Jie, who is said to have lost the Mandate of Heaven, which gave him the right to rule, because of his corrupt and selfish behavior. According to ancient chroniclers, this was the reason why the Xia dynasty collapsed.

Modern scholars are cautious about accepting such claims at face value, though. There are, after all, quite a few examples in ancient times of one civilization conquering or overtaking another and then

---

[3] Min, Anchee. *China: People, Place, Culture, History*. 2007. Pg. 237.

retroactively creating a mythologized account that condemns their predecessors while justifying their own usurpation. It is rare to find honest historical accounts in which a conquering nation or tribe actually states they wanted more territory to add to their power. It was (and still is) standard practice to make the conquered nation out to be the bad guy.

If you rewind ancient Chinese history far enough, the lines begin to blur. However, by the time of the Shang dynasty, a much clearer picture begins to form. The Shang dynasty is said to have begun in 1600 BCE, and it ended around 1046 BCE. The Shang dynasty marks an important period in Chinese history, for it was at this time that the Chinese first began to think of themselves as a polity with a unique purpose.

The notion of China being the "Middle Kingdom," located at the heart of the world, began to take shape. Call it delusions of grandeur or perhaps just wishful thinking, but the idea of the Middle Kingdom states that China is at the center of it all, with the rest of the world revolving around it. The Shang dynasty might seem more than a little boastful in making these proclamations, but its rulers had a good reason to be so proud.

The Chinese under the Shang dynasty pushed the boundaries of the known world. Rulers and court astronomers tracked Mars, comets, and celestial events using inscribed oracle bones, hinting at an early scientific curiosity. Their chariots thundered across the battlefield, wielded by a class of warriors armed with gleaming bronze spears, axes, dagger-axes, and composite bows.

Bronze was the Shang's signature metal. It was used not only for warfare but also for rituals. Elaborate bronze vessels—gū goblets, jué pouring cups, and ding cauldrons—were cast with stunning precision and adorned with mythic motifs. These objects were used in ancestor worship and sacrificial rites. They were often inscribed with clan marks or short dedications. While everyday tools were still made from stone, shell, or wood, the presence of bronze objects—even if reserved for rituals or the elite—shows the Shang dynasty's ability to mobilize resources and skilled labor on an impressive scale.[4]

---

[4] Min, Anchee. *China: People, Place, Culture, History.* Pg. 83.

The Houmuwu ding, made in the 12th century during the late Shang period. This is the largest Bronze Age bronzeware that has been found anywhere in the world. It weighs almost two thousand pounds.[4]

However, perhaps the most important thing for Chinese history was the invention of writing. Archaeologists have dug up bones that contain inscriptions with Chinese characters. Referred to as "oracle bones," it is believed these artifacts were used as a form of divination.

The Shang period also crafted the first major form of religion in China by recognizing Shangdi. According to ancient Chinese tradition, Shangdi was said to have been a divine figure and the ruler of the universe. The concept of Shangdi had a monotheistic bent, even though there were lesser supernatural forces acknowledged in the Chinese pantheon. However, none could compare to Shangdi. Later Christian missionaries referred to the Christian God of the Bible as Shangdi in order to make the religion more appealing to the Chinese. Such tactics were common enough among Christians and had been carried out in other times and places.

The Chinese who revered Shangdi placed sacrifices of food, wine, and other items on altars. They did this not just out of reverence but also out of fear. They thought that if they did not constantly place sacrifices on their altars to appease Shangdi, a calamity (such as a great flood) might happen. And when things got really bad, such as in times of great crisis and upheaval, human beings were sacrificed on the altar of Shangdi in the hopes that it would stave off disaster.

The oracle bones demonstrated more than just contemplation of the heavens. The oracle bones left a clear testament to the Shang rulers' earthly power. The names of various rulers of the Shang dynasty were inscribed on these bones. When archaeologists dug up these bones, they were able to cross-check the inscribed names with later written records to verify both the authenticity of the bones and the authenticity of the preserved, written chronology of the Shang emperors.

At one point in time, the Shang dynasty had its naysayers. There were those who believed that the Shang dynasty was also, or at least partially, a product of ancient myth-making. The oracle bones prove otherwise.

The Shang dynasty was ultimately overtaken by the Zhou dynasty. The Zhou had their own complex ideas on religion and political leadership. These ideas coalesced into the concept of the Mandate of Heaven, the notion that political leaders have been given a mandate from the heavens to rule. The Zhou kickstarted a line of divine rulers who were known as the "Sons of Heaven" or "Tianzi."

During this period, the Chinese believed their own earthly ruler basically served as a bridge between the affairs of mortal humans and the heavens. The Zhou insisted that the Shang rulers had ended their reign due to their own corruption. They believed the Shang rulers had failed in what should have been their most important role—a divine intermediary. The Zhou claimed they would be able to fulfill that role and bring peace and order to the land.

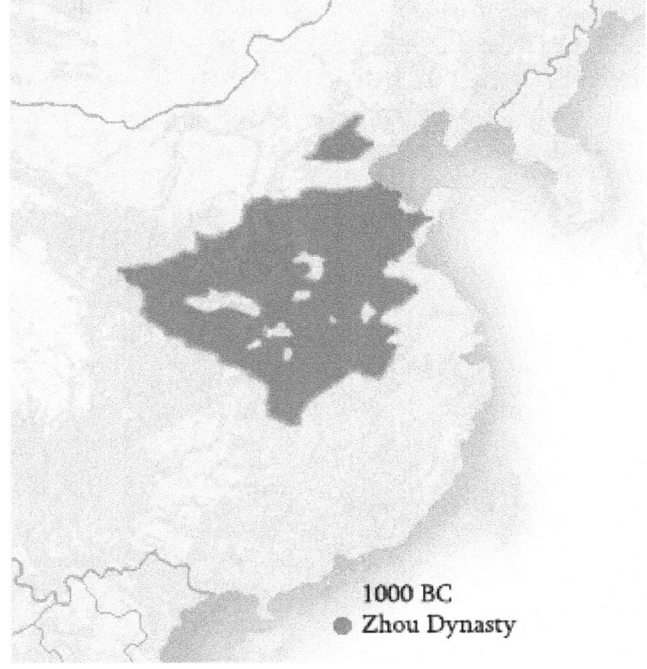

The Zhou dynasty in 1000 BCE.[5]

The aspirations of the Zhou were indeed great, as they desired to have an expansive empire with a strong centralized rule. But as much as they might have desired this kind of arrangement, the reality was far different. The Zhou dynasty was more of a confederation of feudal polities than a unified realm with a strong central government. Local leaders did see the Zhou ruler as their overlord and paid homage to him, but they otherwise lorded over their little corners of the kingdom on their own accord.

The Zhou dynasty eventually began to unravel in the 5th century BCE. Lesser lords, no longer content to pay tribute or defer to the Zhou monarch, began asserting more and more power for themselves. As these regional powers clashed for dominance, China descended into a brutal and prolonged conflict known as the Warring States period.

It was during this time of chaos and uncertainty that a man named Confucius emerged. Arguably China's greatest philosopher, Confucius started out as a keen observer of society. He looked around at the disorder and sought a solution. His answer? Restore harmony through a strict moral code and clearly defined social roles. He believed that everyone had a place, from rulers to servants, and that peace would come when people acted with virtue and fulfilled their duties.

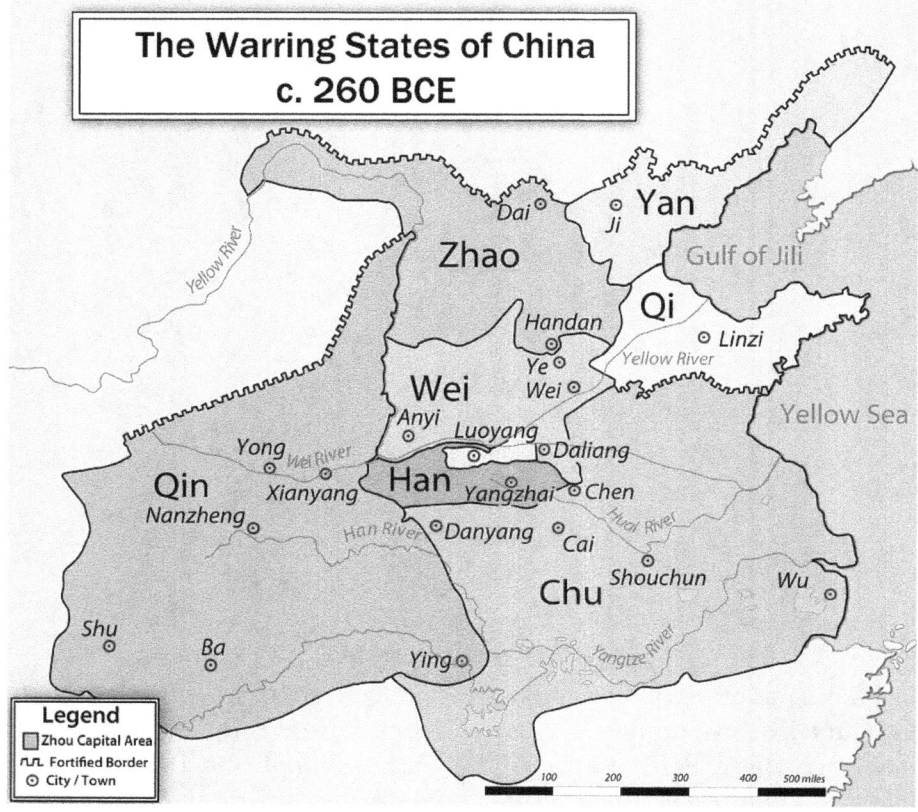

The Warring States period.⁶

After centuries of warfare, one state rose above the rest. The Qin, led by a determined and ruthless ruler named Zhao Zheng, began conquering its rivals one by one. Zhao Zheng had become king of Qin at a young age following the death of his father, King Zhuangxiang, in 246 BCE. Because of his youth, power initially rested in the hands of a regent named Lu Buwei. That didn't last, though. Lu Buwei fell from grace after being caught up in a scandal; he was reportedly involved in an affair with the queen dowager.

Zhao Zheng eventually took full control and proved to be a master of statecraft and war. By 221 BCE, he had succeeded in unifying the warring states under a single ruler. He declared himself Qin Shi Huangdi—"First Emperor of Qin"—and founded a new dynasty.

Qin Shi Huangdi's regime didn't follow Confucian ideals. Instead, it embraced a strict philosophy known as Legalism. Legalist thinkers, especially Han Fei, argued that people could not be trusted to behave morally on their own. Only through harsh laws, strict punishments, and total control could order be maintained. This approach fit well with the authoritarian style of the emperor, who was not shy about using force to get his way.

Under Qin rule, sweeping reforms were introduced. There were standardized weights and measures, a unified script, a national road system, and the early construction of the Great Wall. However, the Qin dynasty's harshness also led to unrest. After Qin Shi Huangdi's death, rebellions erupted, and by 202 BCE, the dynasty was overthrown. In its place rose the Han dynasty, which would go on to rule for centuries and take a much more balanced view between Confucian morality and state power.

Chapter 3: Silk and the Sword

"Soldiers are the foundation of an army; unless they are imbued with a progressive political spirit, and unless such a spirit is fostered through progressive political work, it will be impossible to achieve genuine unity between officers and men, impossible to arouse their enthusiasm for the war of resistance to the full, and impossible to provide an excellent basis for the most effective use of all of our technical equipment and tactics."

-Mao Zedong[5]

Liu Bang's rise is the ultimate underdog story. Born into a peasant family in Pei County and once serving as a low-level law enforcer, few could have predicted his ascent. His leap from obscurity began when, as a Qin prison supervisor, he let prisoners escape rather than let them die under draconian laws. He fled with them, becoming an outlaw, although he eventually returned to Pei. One legend even tells how he slew a great white serpent on the road, which convinced villagers he was destined for greatness.

Fast forward a bit, and he attended the "Feast at Swan Goose Gate" in 206 BCE. This banquet was a trap set by his rival, Xiang Yu. Liu Bang slipped out alive, thanks to a mix of luck, nerves, and quick thinking.

The three-way struggle for China's future culminated in the Battle of Gaixia in 202 BCE, where Liu Bang, aided by brilliant generals like Han Xin, crushed Xiang Yu and emerged as the uncontested master of the realm. He then founded the Han dynasty.

---

[5] Zedong, Mao. *Quotations from Chairman Mao Tse-Tung (The Little Red Book)*. 1964. Pg. 80.

As emperor, Liu Bang did something unexpected. He blended strict Legalist methods with the gentler tones of Confucian thought. Though initially inclined toward realism and practicality, he was swayed by Confucian advisers like Lu Jia to soften punishments and honor ritual and moral governance. In fact, he even paid tribute to Confucius once, passing through the philosopher's hometown.

Liu Bang eventually made Chang'an, near the banks of the Wei River, his capital. This site was actually near the ruined wreckage of the previous Qin capital, Xianyang. The Han dynasty ended up being quite successful, lasting from 202 BCE to 220 CE. The Silk Road stretched all the way into the depths of the Roman Empire. Roman historian Pliny the Elder once remarked in the 1st century CE about how Roman citizens had become rather fond of the flow of goods from China.

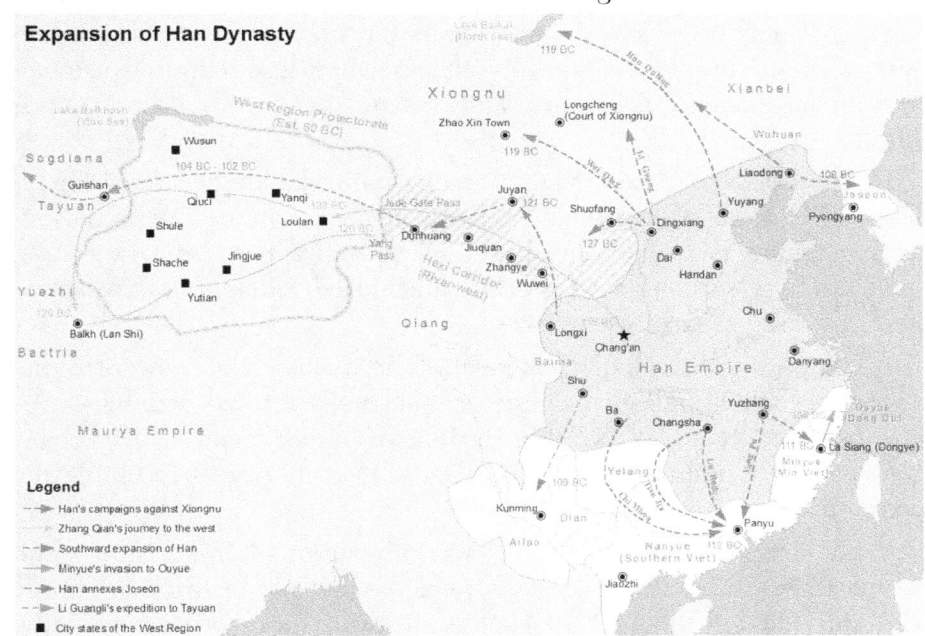

The expansion of the Han dynasty.[7]

It was not always easy going down the Silk Road, though. In 147 BCE, for example, Emperor Wudi of China decided that the merchant classes that profited from the Silk Road had gotten too rich. He decided to curtail the flow of trade down the Silk Road to stop them from gaining more influence and wealth. He also managed to capitalize on the nation's natural resources, making sure that commodities such as iron and salt were used to enrich government coffers.

During the Han dynasty, the Chinese sense of identity really began to crystallize as a distinct and separate entity, set apart from the surrounding peoples. Even today, the majority ethnic group in China is still referred to as "Han" Chinese.

After Emperor Wudi's death, the Han dynasty began its long decline. By the 2nd century CE, cracks were showing in the empire's foundations. The merchant class had grown more powerful, and with that power came greed. Speculation, especially over grain, spun out of control. Prices soared, the ordinary people suffered, and social unrest began bubbling beneath the surface.

But the problems were not just economic. While the Han were dealing with turmoil at home, the empire's northern frontier was under constant threat. Nomadic groups—first the Xiongnu, then the rising Xianbei—launched repeated raids across the borders. These incursions were more than just hit-and-run attacks; they also exposed China's growing vulnerability. Once firm and feared, the Han's military grip was slipping.

In this storm of instability, the Great Wall of China became a line of defense. The wall itself actually predates the Han dynasty. As far back as the 7th century BCE, villagers had built primitive barriers to keep out raiders. These early walls were crude and varied widely, but they served their purpose, at least for a while.

It was not until 221 BCE, under the Qin dynasty, that officials began to connect and standardize these regional walls into something larger. The Han picked up where the Qin left off and expanded the project dramatically. Under their rule, the Great Wall began to resemble the iconic structure we recognize today.

Wall sections were built using a combination of brick, stone, and compacted earth. The outer layers were often made of brick, while the core was filled with tightly packed soil. Even more crucial were the watchtowers, which were spaced at regular intervals along the wall's length. These towers allowed sentries to keep a sharp eye on the horizon. They were ready to light signal fires at the first sign of trouble.

Still, walls alone could not save an empire. However, the Han dynasty's real undoing came from within, not from outside. The economy was off-balance, the pressure on the frontier was constant, and the government was losing its grip. By the late 2nd century CE, those major cracks turned into full fractures. The Yellow Turban Rebellion broke out in 184 CE. This was a massive uprising led by desperate peasants and disillusioned commoners. Though the rebellion was crushed, it left the empire broken. In the years that followed, palace intrigues, corruption, and power struggles tore the court apart.

By 220 CE, the Han dynasty had finally fallen. The emperor was little more than a figurehead, and warlords had carved China into their own personal territories.

This is a pattern that has been repeated throughout Chinese history. Centralized power holds for a time, only to give way to regional fragmentation and civil war. From the fall of the Han to the rise of the Chinese Communist Party in the 20th century, this cycle—unity, decline, disunity, and reunification—has played out again and again.

In any case, as it pertained to the Han dynasty, centralized power broke down, and various regional powers began to duke it out. The powerbrokers of this struggle were warlords with their own regional armies, which they used to exert their will. Among them was a warlord by the name of Cao Cao. He seized control of much of northern China and laid the foundation for the Cao Wei state. He was an intriguing figure who knew as much about poetry as he did war.

Cao Cao actually began his career as a court insider of the Han dynasty. At one point, he even served as security chief under the Han, giving him great insight into the security apparatus of the Han state. He consolidated a lot of power toward the end of the Han dynasty, forging his own army of loyal troops. By the 190s, Han Emperor Xian had basically become a puppet of Cao Cao, making him a mere figurehead.

As what was left of the core of the old Han dynasty stumbled forward, Cao Cao made a name for himself. His greatest success was the unification of northern China, which he brought about in 207 CE. This unified region of northern China would become Cao Cao's personal fief, with Cao Cao essentially becoming a regional warlord, based out of this part of China, before his own passing in March of 220 CE.

His son, Cao Pi, went even further, kickstarting the short-lived Wei dynasty based in the region of northern China that his father had subdued. It was short-lived because shortly after Cao Pi was declared the supreme leader of China (forcing Emperor Xian to abdicate), two rival warlords rose up—one in the interior of China and the other in the south. These three kingdoms were Cao Wei, Shu Han, and Eastern Wu. This era came to be known as the Three Kingdoms period—one of the most legendary and turbulent times in Chinese history. It was a time of almost constant conflict, as each kingdom vied for control over a fractured China.

Each of these kingdoms had its strengths, but none could gain the upper hand for very long. War was relentless, and countless lives were lost in the pursuit of dominance. Plots, betrayals, and last-minute reversals were the norm. If this sounds like something straight out of a novel, that is because it later became one. *Romance of the Three Kingdoms* was one of China's most famous works of historical fiction, and it immortalized this era.

After decades of stalemates, one kingdom finally pulled ahead: Cao Wei. However, just when it seemed poised to reunite China, its own internal power struggles led to its undoing. A powerful general named Sima Yan eventually usurped the throne. In 266 CE, he founded a new dynasty called the Jin.

The Jin dynasty conquered Eastern Wu by 280 CE, finally reuniting the country after nearly a century of division. For a brief moment, it looked like peace had returned.

The Jin dynasty in 280 CE.⁸

However, we should keep in mind that one has to be careful when speaking of the Jin dynasty since there has been more than one of them during the course of China's history. About a thousand years after this first Jin dynasty, another one would rise up. This second one is often referred to as the Jurchen Jin dynasty to avoid confusion.

Just a few years after China was unified, the dynasty was dragged into a devastating internal conflict known as the War of the Eight Princes. As the dynasty tore itself apart from the inside, opportunistic groups from the north and west began pouring into China's heartland. These groups—often referred to as the Five Barbarians—included nomadic tribes like the Xiongnu, Xianbei, Di, Jie, and Qiang. They had been living along the borders for generations, sometimes under Chinese control. With the empire distracted, they seized their moment. Some rebelled, and others carved out their own small kingdoms.

In 311 CE, one of these groups stormed the Jin capital of Luoyang in what became known as the Disaster of Yongjia. The city was burned, its people were massacred, and the imperial tombs were looted. A few years later, in 316, the emperor was captured and executed. The Western Jin dynasty was over.

However, the dynasty was not quite finished. Members of the Jin royal family who survived fled south, regrouped, and set up a new capital in Jiankang—modern-day Nanjing. This was the start of the Eastern Jin dynasty. While they never recovered the northern territories, the Eastern Jin held on in the south for another century, although it was not easy. The court was riddled with intrigue. Generals and ministers constantly jockeyed for control. Still, they managed a few major victories, most notably the Battle of Fei River in 383 CE, where a much smaller Jin force defeated a powerful northern invader and saved the south from conquest.

Even the Eastern Jin could not hold on. A general named Liu Yu rose through the ranks. He outmaneuvered his rivals and took the throne in 420. He ended the Jin dynasty and started one of his own: the Liu Song dynasty. China once again slipped into a familiar pattern of rival dynasties in the north and south, each claiming legitimacy but unable to fully defeat the other.

Nearly a century later, something changed. In the south, a new emperor came to power: Emperor Wu of the Liang dynasty, who ruled from 502 to 549. He was different. Raised in the traditions of

Confucianism, he later became one of China's greatest Buddhist patrons. Known as the Bodhisattva Emperor, he poured resources into temples, encouraged the spread of Buddhist teachings, and even abolished the death penalty for a time. Under his reign, the south experienced a rare moment of peace and cultural flourishing.

It would not last forever—nothing ever does in history—but for a brief time, it looked like China might find balance again.

The fact that Buddhism took root in China is interesting. On the surface, many of the tenets of Buddhism seem incompatible with the social template provided by Confucianism. Buddhism focuses on seeking the salvation of the individual, paying no heed to social and familial ties, whereas social and family hierarchy are of great importance in Confucianism. So, how did Buddhism manage to find such fertile ground in China?

The fact that China had been politically fractured for so long likely had a lot to do with it. There was no strong Confucian-oriented polity for much of this period that could have better resisted the pull of Buddhism. Instead, in this time of chaos and upheaval, the Buddhist ideals of empowering oneself to find spiritual freedom had likely become very appealing to the people.

Another interesting aspect was that the Buddhist example of monastic life became preferable during war and violence since the monastery represented a refuge of peace and security. Religious seekers, as well as intellectuals of all kinds, found a safe and welcoming environment among the Buddhists.

Buddhist monasteries eventually became more than just religious centers. They were also educational centers, safeguarding Chinese intellectual thought and culture. The manner in which Buddhist monasteries became centers of education during these troubling times in China's history has some historical parallels. The safeguarding of knowledge in Buddhist monasteries is very similar to the way in which Christian monasteries served as beacons of spiritual and intellectual light during the European Dark Ages. As the warlords duked it out during this troubling period in China, the safest place to deposit books, manuscripts, inventions, or any other notable ideas was likely in a Buddhist monastery.

The Hanging Monastery in Shanxi Province.[9]

Out of this tumult came the Sui dynasty, which was briefly prominent, lasting from 581 to 618. The Sui dynasty was a mere speedbump in the long history of China, but it was important all the same. Under the Sui, the rulers again unified China. Although the dynasty lasted fewer than forty years, it laid out the framework for a much more successful dynasty: the Tang.

Chapter 4: From the Tang to the Song

"Life is really simple, but men insist on making it complicated."
-Confucius[6]

The great Emperor Gaozu founded the Tang dynasty around 618. He was initially struggling for dominance in a competitive field of candidates who were seeking to lead the flailing Sui dynasty. He ultimately put down his rivals, but instead of continuing the Sui dynasty, he forged the Tang dynasty instead. The Tang built upon the Sui and managed to create lasting legal codes and government infrastructure.

Emperor Gaozu's government was not a one-man show. It operated through a clever structure known as the Three Departments and Six Ministries. Think of it as a high-functioning administration: one department drafted policy, another reviewed it, and a third carried it out. Meanwhile, the six ministries—personnel (handling appointments), revenue (managing taxes and finance), rites (dealing with ceremonies and protocols), war (military affairs), justice (law and order), and works (infrastructure)—handled the day-to-day running of the empire.

Now, about the royal drama. Gaozu's two most formidable sons were Li Jiancheng, the crown prince, and Li Shimin, the warrior prince. Unlike Li Jiancheng, who spent much of his time stationed on the

---

[6] Brewer, D. *Quotes of Confucius and Their Interpretations: A Words of Wisdom Collection Book.* Pg. 39.

frontier, Li Shimin was the empire's hero, defeating key rivals and commanding respect from the army. The competition between them was fierce, and it eventually boiled over into open violence.

In 626, that tension came to a head in what's now known as the Xuanwu Gate Incident. Li Shimin set an ambush at the palace's northern gate and assassinated Li Jiancheng and their brother, Li Yuanji. It was quick, brutal, and effective. Within days, Emperor Gaozu had no choice but to make Li Shimin the crown prince, and soon after, he abdicated in his favor.

Li Shimin became Emperor Taizong, and he went on to become one of China's greatest rulers. Taizong was known to have greatly projected Chinese power. He managed to expand his territory and create satellite vassals out of neighboring countries. He even made inroads in the Tarim Basin, reaching into central Asia. Here, the Tang managed to bring the Uyghurs and Turkish nomads to heel, thereby securing the Silk Road.

Interestingly, Emperor Taizong's sister, Princess Pingyang, is said to have played a big role in all of this. She was apparently skilled in the art of war. In what was most certainly an unusual development back in those days, Princess Pingyang actually led her own battalion of troops, which was known as the Army of the Lady. This army was able to conquer a few territories of strategic importance. Princess Pingyang was then able to unite her forces with those of Emperor Taizong.

It is not entirely clear what happened to Princess Pingyang, but it is said that she perished while in her twenties in 623. Demonstrating how important she was to the Chinese war effort (not to mention how important she was to her brother), the princess was given a military burial similar to what would have been given to an accomplished male general.

This security brought more trade, and with it came a whole lot more traffic. Soon, many outsiders were flocking to China, creating a cosmopolitan feel in many Chinese cities. The influence of the Tang even managed to reach Japan, which began to actively emulate China.

China and Tibet also began to develop a close relationship around this time. Their relationship revolved around the trade of tea and horses. It sounds rather simple, and from a commerce perspective, it is. After all, China wanted horses and Tibet wanted tea. The trade route that carved its way through China into the highlands of Tibet was known as the Tea Horse Road. Of course, tea and horses were not the only things that traveled along this road. As Chinese culture mingled with Tibetan life, Buddhism took root and began to reshape Tibetan spiritual practices.

Emperor Taizong died in 649 CE, leaving the throne to his son, Gaozong. On paper, the new ruler had all the makings of a worthy successor—he had years as crown prince and a fine education, plus the Tang dynasty was at its height. Yet in the eyes of later chroniclers, Gaozong was a shadow of his father. They painted him as hesitant, pliable, and all too easily swayed by his brilliant and ambitious consort, Wu Zetian, a woman who had once served as Taizong's concubine. That single fact was enough for later storytellers to cast his reign as ineffective, turning a court romance into a political cautionary tale.

However, this was not just mere slander because his taking up with Wu Zetian did have a big impact on his reign. Even though Gaozong was already married, this concubine managed to become Gaozong's favorite. Demonstrating a more powerful sense of willpower than Gaozong could muster, she managed to convince him to recognize her as more or less an equal.

As such, this former concubine became the infamous Empress Wu, and soon she—not Gaozong—was the true power behind the throne. Gaozong eventually became incapacitated by a stroke, and Empress Wu served as his "interpreter." No one could understand the stricken Gaozong but the empress. This was very convenient for her, although it was inconvenient for everyone else. She basically made Gaozong her own feeble puppet. Empress Wu could propose any policy she wanted. During these dark days, she made sure that her and Gaozong's son were established as the heirs to the throne, thereby ensuring her own hold on the Tang dynasty.

Although Gaozong's reign was troubled, the empire was still strong thanks to his predecessor. The Tang Empire had expanded geographically, absorbing plenty of additional resources. The army had also expanded and was a formidable fighting force, no matter who was on the throne.

In fact, the military might of China beckoned a horde of refugees from Persia (modern-day Iran) who were fleeing from the Islamic conquest. The Persians had an ancient empire; by the 7th century, the empire already stretched back thousands of years. However, at the start of Gaozong's reign, Persia was overwhelmed by the determined and ideologically empowered Arab army. Persian defenses were ultimately overrun.

After the fall of the Sasanian Empire in 651, members of the royal Persian family fled east, seeking refuge from the Arab conquest. Among them was Peroz, a son of the last Sasanian king, Yazdegerd III. He made his way to Tang China, where he and other Persian nobles were welcomed by the emperor and granted titles and protection.

Some later stories even claim that one of Yazdegerd's daughters entered the Tang imperial court, possibly as a concubine to Emperor Taizong, though this part of the tale is steeped more in legend than documented fact.

Under Tang protection, Peroz lived out his days in the Chinese borderlands. Though he likely harbored dreams of one day returning to reclaim his homeland, that dream never materialized. Over time, the Persian refugees chose to settle, raise families, and gradually integrate into Chinese society. It is said that near the end of his life, Peroz advised his people to honor their Persian roots while embracing the land that had sheltered them.

And so they did. Over generations, through intermarriage and cultural exchange, this Persian community became woven into the broader fabric of Chinese civilization. Today, only subtle traces remain.

Emperor Gaozong died in 683, and just as Empress Wu had arranged, the heir was her son with Gaozong, Zhongzong. If she expected a pliable figurehead, she was soon disappointed. When Zhongzong began to assert himself, favoring his wife's family over Empress Wu's influence, she moved swiftly. She deposed him after barely six weeks and installed her younger son, Ruizong, on the throne. Empress Wu ruled in all but name.

For years, she kept up the appearance of Tang rule, but in 690, she cast aside the pretense. She declared herself emperor and made the empire her own. She served as the sole authority of China over the next fifteen years. Even though Empress Wu is widely reviled in traditional Chinese history, one could argue that she was, in fact, a fairly decent ruler. Yes, her climb to power was ruthless, but she played the game of politics remarkably well. Rising from concubine to emperor, she inherited a shaky dynasty and turned it into a flourishing one. She got rid of corruption, expanded the empire, rejuvenated the economy, and transformed the civil service so that ability, not birth, became the measure of a man.

Just before her death in 705, Wu Zetian was forced by illness and palace intrigue to reinstate her son Zhongzong. However, Zhongzong's second go at ruling would not work out very well at all. Zhongzong's death in 710 CE was sudden and widely believed to be no accident. Traditional historians say Empress Wei, backed by her daughter Princess Anle, poisoned him with a cake. She wanted to follow the path of previous empresses and seize true power herself. With the emperor gone, Wei enthroned his young son, Li Chongmao, hoping he would be a puppet under her thumb.

However, this was not how things played out. Within two weeks, a coup led by Zhongzong's sister, Princess Taiping, and Li Dan's son, the future Xuanzong, overthrew Empress Wei. Ruizong, Zhongzong's brother, was put on the throne, and the coup plotters were executed.

Emperor Xuanzong would have a much more stable rule than his immediate predecessors. He led the dynasty from 712 to 756; his reign was the longest among the Tang emperors. However, his reign was not without its problems. Middle Eastern armies, fueled by the fervor of Islam, were on the march. Persia had already been knocked out, and now Islamic ideologues were hammering at China's own western borderlands.

Emperor Xuanzong's later years took an unexpected turn. His most cherished companion was Consort Wu, a great-niece of the formidable Empress Wu Zetian. When she died suddenly in 737, Xuanzong was inconsolable. In his grief, his affections turned to an unlikely figure: the young wife of his own son, Prince Shou. To make the match possible, she briefly donned Taoist robes to dissolve her marriage. Then, she returned to the palace as Yang Guifei.

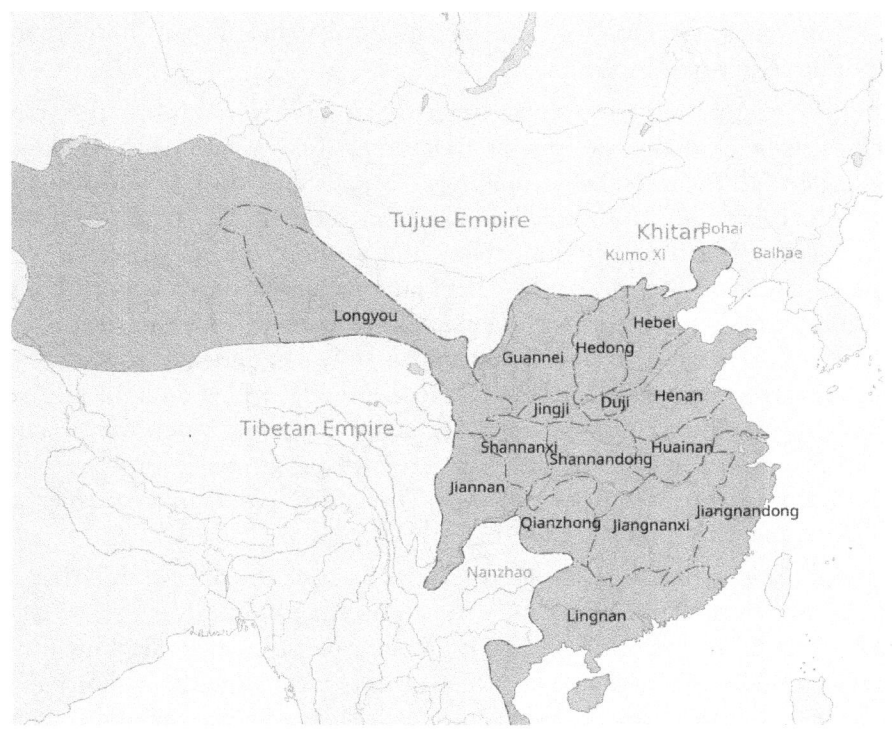

The Tang dynasty in the early 740s.[10]

The Tang army was in for a stunning defeat. In 751, an Arab army from the Abbasid Caliphate confronted Tang forces near the banks of the Talas River, which flows through Kyrgyzstan and Kazakhstan. For the Tang, the battle would mark the end of their western ambitions. Midway through the fight, their Turkic Karluk allies—said to number some twenty thousand—suddenly turned their lances against the Chinese, joining their Muslim brethren in crushing the Tang. When the dust settled, the Abbasids held the field, and Tang influence beyond the Tian Shan, a mountain range in central Asia, was gone for good.

This was a stunning blow to China. The real shock came in 755 when General An Lushan rose up in rebellion and seized both of the Tang capitals. Xuanzong fled for his life. In the chaos, his son, Li Heng, was proclaimed Emperor Suzong in the north. Xuanzong formally abdicated, though he still issued decrees for a short while.

With the empire on the brink of collapse, Suzong made a desperate but effective move. He called in the Uyghur Khaganate. These mounted warriors answered the call and helped the Tang army reclaim Chang'an and Luoyang in late 757. This alliance saved the dynasty, but it came at a cost. Suzong's reliance on foreign troops revealed just how fragile imperial power had become.

The Uyghurs had recently accepted Islam and were among the many warring tribes on the steppes at that time. The Uyghurs were skilled warriors, even on horseback, making them a highly mobile and valuable strike force to the Chinese. The Uyghurs helped the Chinese retake some lost territories, but in exchange for their efforts, thousands of Uyghurs were allowed to settle in the far reaches of northwestern China in what today is referred to as Xiangjiang province. Both the region and the Uyghurs themselves have been in the news headlines of more recent times due to accusations that the Chinese are attempting a cultural (if not a literal) genocide against the Uyghurs. They have forbidden the practice of Islam and forced the Uyghurs to adopt Chinese customs and ideological beliefs. There is still much debate on what may or may not be taking place in Xiangjiang.

China might have managed to secure its borders during this period, but more internal problems were to come. China entered into what is historically known as the Late Tang Weak Monsoon Period. This was a roughly one-hundred-year-long cycle of extreme drought, which led to crop failures. As is often the case, during this time of crisis, the social order broke down, and rebellions and insurrections became frequent.

In 878, the Chinese rebel leader Huang Chao launched a devastating uprising against the Tang dynasty. Part of his anger was channeled toward foreign communities—Muslims, Jews, Christians, and Zoroastrians—who became scapegoats for China's troubles. Huang's forces stormed Guangzhou. Historians from the Persian Gulf estimated that tens of thousands of foreigners were slaughtered, though Chinese records are quieter about the numbers.

Huang's rebellion shook the empire to its core. Eventually, the Tang court enlisted new military talent, most notably the Shatuo leader Li Keyong, to crush the rebellion. By 884, Huang had been defeated, but the dynasty was a shadow of its former self. Over the following decades, regional military governors gained influence, and the central authority continued to weaken until the Tang dynasty finally ended in 907.

Out of that chaos, the Five Dynasties and Ten Kingdoms period began. It was not until 960 that peace—and a new dynasty—returned. Zhao Kuangyin, later Emperor Taizu of the Song, rose to unify the realm and establish the Song dynasty, which would endure until 1279.

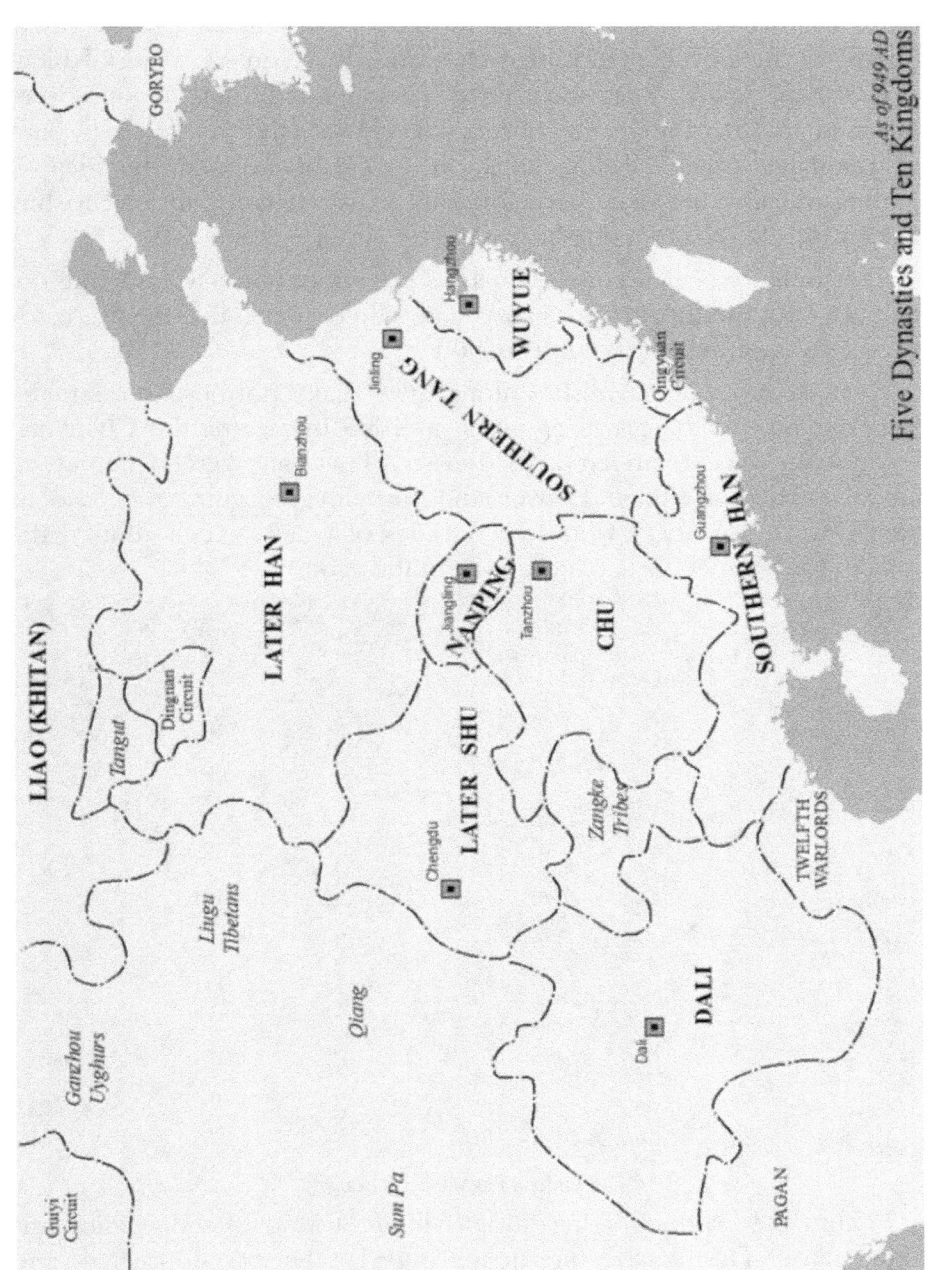

A map of China during the Five Dynasties and Ten Kingdoms period.[11]

The Song dynasty was shaped in no small part by the nomadic warriors of the northern steppes. Their influence was both direct and indirect. Once the empire was unified under Zhao Kuangyin, its rulers looked to the north, determined to secure the frontier against Khitan and Tangut raids. Garrisons were strengthened, and troops were stationed in force along the borders. However, this was a costly and unsustainable policy. Before long, the Song abandoned the idea of holding the line through sheer force of arms, choosing instead to buy peace with silk, silver, and gold.

This practice is also not sustainable. The more you pay someone not to attack you, the more threats and attacks there are so that the aggressor can get an even bigger payout from you.

After decades of skirmishes along their shaky northern border, the Song dynasty finally agreed to peace in 1005 by signing the Chanyuan Treaty with the Khitan-led Liao dynasty. The Song agreed to pay an annual tribute of silk and silver and formally recognize the Liao as equals. In return, there would be decades of peace, which allowed the Song to focus on culture, education, and the economy.

The Leifeng Pagoda by Li Song.[12]

Within the borders of the Song dynasty, a kind of renaissance was taking place. Despite the turbulence outside, the arts flourished, and there were innovative inventions of all kinds. The Song Empire developed a practical military use of gunpowder, refined the compass, and issued true paper money (a first in world history). The Song also greatly expanded the civil service, creating a complex bureaucracy. Those interested in civil service positions had to take exams. They had to demonstrate their ability to write essays, their knowledge of Confucian principles, and even write their own poetry. This introduced the idea that one could rise through the ranks by way of merit. One's background was important, but if one could not apply practical knowledge to their position, then they were not the right candidate.

It was a nice idea, but much of the time, it did not actually work in practice. There was still an awful lot of corruption, which served to aid some over others. There were also segments of the Chinese population who were illiterate, such as laborers or farmers, who simply did not have the education necessary to take a civil examination in the first place. Nevertheless, the Chinese civil service and its exams were a unique and forward-thinking innovation at the time.

During the Song dynasty, China developed a great passion for theater. Playhouses popped up in just about every city, and actors portrayed dramas of all kinds.

None of these dramas could compete with the very real drama taking shape in China's northern frontier. As northern China became less prosperous and more unpredictable, southern China (later known as the Southern Song dynasty) rose to prominence. In the south, rice and tea were produced in large quantities. This led to a shift away from the previous diet of mostly grains to one centered around the foodstuffs of southern China. Rice could be grown in the warm climate of southern China and then shipped via waterways to the major cities farther north, keeping everyone well fed.

In the early 1100s, the Song struck a risky bargain with the rising Jurchens. Together, they would crush the Khitan Liao dynasty. The Jin dynasty, as the Jurchens styled themselves, swept the Khitans from the map by 1125 and then turned their armies south. In 1127, they stormed the Song capital at Kaifeng, carrying off the emperor and his court in what became known as the Jingkang Incident. The Northern Song was gone. The remnants of the dynasty fled south, eventually establishing a new capital at Hangzhou. From there, the Southern Song would endure for another century and a half until the Mongols came to finish its story in 1279.

Ever since their great progenitor Genghis Khan rose to prominence in Mongolia in 1206, the Mongols had been on the march. His grandson, Kublai Khan, would defeat Song China and establish a unified China under his own rule, which would become known as the Yuan dynasty. Although the Yuan dynasty was a Mongol creation, it did what it could to replicate the achievements of the Song.

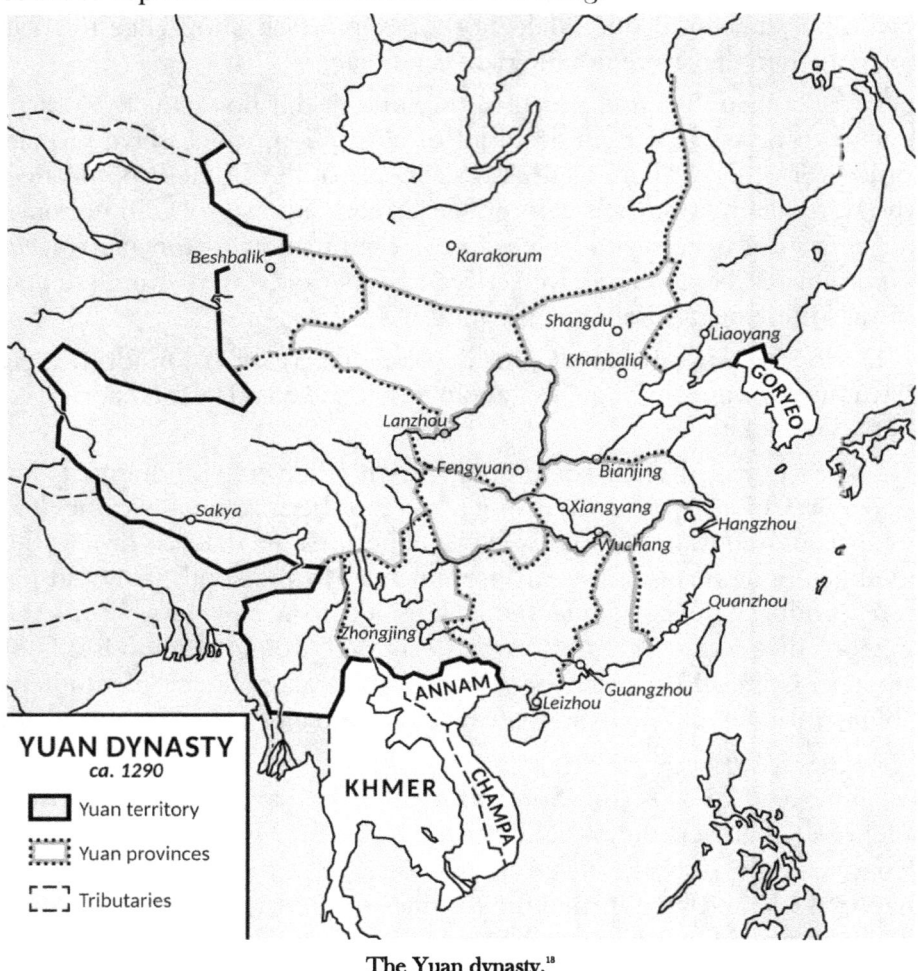

The Yuan dynasty.[18]

The Mongols took advantage of Song achievements, such as paper money and gunpowder. Despite their fearsome reputation, the Mongols were not necessarily malevolent overlords. Life for most Chinese went on as usual. Even so, there was growing resentment over the fact that China was being run by outsiders.

The Chinese soon began moving toward open revolt against their Mongol rulers. During this time of duress, many delved into mysticism and prophecy, seeking a sign that an intervention against the Mongols might be at hand. Although it is debatable what this "sign" could be, there was one incident in particular that stood out.

In the 1350s, China was battered by harsh climates, crop failures, floods, cyclones, famine, and possibly even plague. Disillusioned and desperate, the people yearned for a sign that the Yuan dynasty had lost the Mandate of Heaven. Out of this storm rose a movement that combined spirituality with politics: the Red Turban Rebellion. It was named for the red headbands tied by White Lotus-inspired sectarians preaching a coming savior.

Starting around 1351, figures like Han Shantong began rallying corvée laborers and peasants under the banner of divine restoration and anti-Mongol revolt. Though it was, for the most part, crushed early on, the movement ultimately coalesced around Zhu Yuanzhang, a charismatic general who defeated the Yuan armies and outmaneuvered rival warlords. His stunning naval victory at Lake Poyang in 1363 sealed his dominance and paved the way for the founding of the Ming dynasty in 1368.

The chaos even spilled into Goryeo (present-day Korea), where Red Turban forces raided Pyongyang, although they were pushed back by local armies. By that point, the Yuan dynasty had little left to stand on. By the time Zhu Yuanzhang declared himself emperor, China had been reshaped through rebellion, faith, and the relentless force of a peasant army.

Chapter 5: The Majesty of the Ming Dynasty

"In seeking victory, those who direct a war cannot overstep the limitations imposed by the objective conditions. Within these limitations, however, they can and must play a dynamic role in striving for victory. The stage of action for commanders in a war must be built upon objective possibilities, but on that stage they can direct the performance of many a drama, full of sound and color, power and grandeur."

-*Mao Zedong*[7]

    The revolt that pushed the Mongols out of China was led by Zhu Yuanzhang. Zhu was an unlikely hero in many respects, and he was most certainly an unlikely leader. He was an orphan and had lived most of his life as a homeless vagabond. He eventually adopted Buddhism and depended upon the kindness of strangers for sustenance.

    During his days as a wandering Buddhist monk, he happened upon a religious and political revival of sorts. This popular revival ultimately morphed into the Red Turban Rebellion. After driving the Mongols from China, Zhu formed the Ming dynasty, which roughly translates as "bringer of light." Yes, Zhu and his followers saw themselves as bringing light back to China. They restored order, virtue, and Chinese traditions after what they viewed as years of Mongol misrule.

---

[7] Zedong, Mao. *Quotations from Chairman Mao Tse-Tung (The Little Red Book)*. Pg. 124.

To many in China, especially the Confucian elite, the Yuan dynasty had been a dark chapter. China had to deal with foreign overlords, harsh taxes, and a loss of cultural identity. But in truth, the picture was more complicated. The Mongols maintained trade routes, tolerated diverse religions, and brought China into closer contact with the wider world. Even so, for many Chinese at the time, the end of the Yuan dynasty felt like the lifting of a long shadow.

Zhu Yuanzhang became the Hongwu Emperor. He was determined to bring back a renaissance of Chinese culture and innovation, which had been subsumed for so long by the Mongolian occupiers. The Hongwu Emperor also made sure to reestablish protocols with all of China's former tribute nations. He let it be known that he fully expected the leaders of China's traditional satellites to pay their respects to him personally. And they did. The first to arrive was Tran Du Tong, the emperor of Vietnam. Several other leaders from other Southeast Asian nations, such as Cambodia, Majapahit, Borneo, and Sumatra, also sent representatives.

The Hongwu Emperor orchestrated elaborate ceremonies where foreign dignitaries were received with fanfare, hospitality, and no small amount of symbolic power play. These rituals were meant to underscore China's superiority and the emperor's dominance. Visiting rulers were treated with generosity, but it was always clear that any show of disobedience would bring swift consequences.

That message applied not just to foreign emissaries but to internal threats as well. In 1380, the emperor's growing paranoia came to a head when he suspected his own chancellor, Hu Weiyong, of plotting treason. Whether the

Portrait of the Hongwu Emperor.[14]

plot was real or imagined is still debated, but what followed was a purge. Hu Weiyong was executed, and tens of thousands of officials, associates, and even distant contacts were swept up in the fallout. The office of chancellor was abolished, and from that point on, the six ministries reported directly to the emperor. The Hongwu Emperor had consolidated control in a way no Chinese emperor had before.

The emperor's paranoia extended to other parts of court life, especially the palace eunuchs. These castrated men were tasked with guarding the imperial harem since their condition eliminated any risk of scandal with the emperor's concubines. However, the Hongwu Emperor believed that physical barriers were not enough to prevent intrigue. He thought eunuchs could still conspire, especially with concubines who might use their influence for personal or political gain. There were whispers of plots, embezzlement schemes, and interference in state affairs. Whether those rumors were founded or not, Hongwu treated them seriously. In 1385, he issued a sweeping decree. Any eunuch found involved in political plotting would face immediate execution.[8]

As the end of his reign approached, the Hongwu Emperor made a bold dynastic decision. Instead of passing the throne to one of his many surviving sons, he named his young grandson, Zhu Yunwen, as his successor. He would become the Jianwen Emperor, and he came to power in 1398. Still in his teens, the Jianwen Emperor faced a fractured court and a country weary of purges and authoritarian rule. Recognizing this, his first major act as emperor was to issue a general pardon. He released many who had been imprisoned or sidelined under his grandfather's regime, offering clemency to those who had fallen out of favor. This was not just a gesture of goodwill. The Jianwen Emperor needed to stabilize the empire and win loyalty from factions still smarting from the Hongwu Emperor's reign.

But as promising as the Jianwen Emperor's reign had begun, it would end rather abruptly in 1402. The exact way in which the Jianwen Emperor was toppled remains unknown, but we have a general idea. His demise was born out of the animosity of his uncles, who were upset that they had been passed over in the line of succession. They felt that the Hongwu Emperor should never have considered his grandson; they felt that the crown should have first gone to one of the Hongwu Emperor's brothers.

---

[8] Min, Anchee. *China: People, Place, Culture, History.* Pg. 108.

One of these uncles cobbled together a large army and marched on the capital of China, Nanjing. The next thing anyone knew, Jianwen was nowhere to be seen. The uncle who had stormed into Nanjing claimed that he was on a rescue mission to save his nephew from an attempted coup. However, he then claimed that he had failed in his mission and that the young man had been killed; he was apparently burned alive in his own palace. Most could read between the lines of all this and realized that his uncle had killed him. At any rate, this uncle went on to become the Yongle Emperor. He would rule from 1402 to 1424.

The Yongle Emperor was an expansionist and built up the army so that he could fulfill his expansionist ambitions. In 1403, he moved the capital of China to Beijing. Prior to this, Nanjing was considered the capital, but shortly after coming to power, the Yongle Emperor decided that Beijing was of greater strategic importance and would be the better choice for China's capital city. If anything else, he could keep a better watch on the continued threat of Mongol invasion from Beijing.

Shortly after Beijing was designated the capital, construction began on one of China's most noteworthy sites, the Forbidden City. This inner sanctum of Beijing, said to be forbidden because it was the official stomping grounds of the emperor, would not be finalized until the year 1420.

The Yongle Emperor also did everything he could to strengthen the ancient Great Wall of China. The Great Wall had long stood as a barrier between China and invaders. The Yongle Emperor sought to bolster its potential for deterrence and defense as much as possible. In fact, the Great Wall reached its maximum length and came to take on the general design and appearance that the structure is known for today under the Ming.

One of the most endearing legacies of the wall's refurbishment during the Ming era was that towns popped up along the wall due to the tremendous manpower needed to work on the sections. These towns became lasting settlements.

The Yongle Emperor was quite enthusiastic about using the resources and manpower that China already had at its disposal, and this also extended to the Chinese army. In the past, the Chinese had relied heavily on mercenaries. The Yongle Emperor made sure that China had its own homegrown army on which it could depend.

As much as China was seeking to defend its people during this period, it was also embarking on previously unheard-of explorations. During the Ming era, the famed Admiral Zheng He led a fleet of Chinese galleons over the Indian Ocean to tour India, Africa, and everything in between.

Zheng He's first exploratory mission took place from 1405 to 1407. He and his crew traveled past Indochina and down to Java before entering the Indian Ocean. Several more voyages ensued to parts far and wide, which would be remembered by the locals for several decades.

Zheng He's ships are referred to as the "Treasure Fleets," and for good reason. These ships were loaded to the brim with all manner of goods. The Chinese wanted to make sure that they were beholden to no one during these trips, so they supplied these ships with more than just provisions. This put them in a strong position as diplomats since they could arrive at a foreign port bearing gifts and seeking nothing in return. Well, nothing, perhaps, except for a pledge of future diplomatic relations with China from their hosts.

As awed as these local leaders were by the spectacle, they could hardly say that the Chinese were threatening them or stealing their resources. So, what was it that they wanted? It seems that they wanted to spread Chinese worldviews and philosophy, not so much through force but by a gentle diplomatic push.

If this was indeed the goal, one could say that Zheng He's efforts were a stunning success. The few exotic items he returned with were a source of endless amusement and wonder in the Chinese court. For example, Zheng He's ships returned with a rather remarkable animal that most Chinese knew nothing about. They were stunned to see a beast with a tremendously long neck being led out of a ship and out onto the dock. This animal was a giraffe. This particular giraffe originally hailed from Africa but had been picked up in Bengal. The giraffe's arrival in China was well documented by paintings, poems, and chronicles.

Interestingly enough, some Chinese spoke of the animal as somehow being prophetic. This was due to the fact that Chinese myth spoke of a unicorn-like creature that was last seen during the time of Confucius. The giraffe does not really look like a unicorn, but it is possible that some Chinese thought it was weird enough to classify it as one. They insisted that its arrival in China meant that the Chinese had entered into a new and wondrous golden age. There was certainly an optimistic mood in China during the early days of the Ming dynasty.

Zheng He's last voyage ended up on the eastern coast of Africa in an apparent search for the native habitat of exotic animals like the giraffe. Diplomacy was also a part of his agenda, with Zheng He establishing diplomatic relations with regions in Southeast Asia and East Africa. But as interesting and ground-breaking as these trips were, they were determined to be a waste of money since more resources were needed to maintain northern defenses and undertake punitive expeditions against the constant threat of the Mongols.

Emperor Yongle passed away in 1424. His successor allowed one more voyage in 1431 before shutting down the Treasure Fleets for good. European explorers, in the meantime, were ramping up their own efforts at exploration, with the Portuguese leading the charge. The Portuguese would reach India in 1498, and they would reach China itself in 1514.

Just prior to this feat, the Portuguese had forcefully seized the nearby Southeast Asian island of Malacca. Malacca served as a stepping stone to reach China. As daring as the Portuguese were, they were not about to strong-arm China into submission. However, they did engage in a rather aggressive form of diplomacy. After several entreaties by the eager Portuguese, the Chinese finally allowed a Portuguese mission to be established in China's southern port city of Canton.

The Chinese had been using Canton for some time as an official weigh station and to deal with foreign delegations. The Portuguese were viewed as just the latest of these pests, but little did the Chinese know that the Portuguese were playing for keeps. Relations eventually broke down once China discovered rogue Portuguese sailors were basically resorting to piracy in Chinese waters.

These trespasses led to a confrontation between a Ming fleet and a Portuguese fleet in the vicinity of Guangzhou. The Portuguese were thrashed by the Chinese, and in the aftermath, Chinese officials sought to end all relations with them. The persistent Portuguese eventually wormed their way back. In 1554, they managed to gain permission to establish another mission, this time in the Chinese port of Macau. Macau became an official trading post in 1557. The Portuguese were thinking more about the long term than the Chinese would have guessed at the time. Macau would ultimately become a Portuguese colony; it remained a Portuguese possession until 1999.

The Portuguese were not the only Europeans who made inroads in Asia. Their Iberian cousins, the Spaniards, were not far behind. By the late 1500s, the Spaniards had conquered their way across the Americas.

After disembarking from the Pacific coast, they pushed farther west—so far west, in fact, that one could say it became east! They ultimately sailed all the way to the Philippines, which fell under their control as well.

From their base in the Philippines, the Spaniards sailed to China with galleons full of gold and silver freshly purloined from their American conquests. Chinese coffers would become filled with Spanish silver, while Spanish ships were filled with silk and other precious commodities.

As much as European depredations played a role in China's later decline, during this period, China actually had more to fear from Japan. The Japanese certainly could not stand up to Ming China on a one-to-one basis militarily, but for several decades, rogue pirate bands had been plaguing the Chinese coasts. These pirates posed a significant threat to China's resources.

Matters came to a head in 1592 when Japan officially invaded Korea. At the time, Korea was a tributary vassal of China. If China could not protect its own vassal states, no one would look at China as a strong and effective power. If Korea could not count on China's protection, who could?

By the late Ming period, the cracks in the dynasty had begun to show. Years of financial strain, political corruption, and environmental disasters like floods and famines had battered the empire. Though still impressive in size and influence, the Ming government was growing weaker by the decade. The war with Japan in Korea had been a major blow. While China successfully repelled the invaders and preserved its status as protector of the Korean court, the effort drained the treasury and exposed just how fragile the Ming military machine had become.

As Ming control over its vast territories began to slip, the northeastern region of Manchuria grew increasingly independent. The Jurchen tribes of this region—later known as the Manchus—had long existed at the empire's edge. They were sometimes trading partners, but at other times, they were foes. Though they had pledged allegiance to the Ming court in earlier decades, that relationship had grown hollow. By the early 1600s, the Manchus had organized under a charismatic leader named Nurhaci, who united the Jurchen clans and declared the founding of a new state. He soon issued a manifesto—known as the Seven Grievances—which formally accused the Ming of betrayal and declared open war.

Even as the Ming grappled with this threat from the north, its internal foundations were crumbling. Court officials were locked in endless power struggles. The emperor's ear was often captured by eunuchs or self-serving ministers. Rebellions broke out across the countryside as peasants grew desperate and local governors lost control.

And yet, even in this climate of political decay, the cultural life of China remained vibrant. The late Ming period saw a flourishing of art, literature, and philosophy. Painters experimented with bold new styles, and novelists penned some of China's most enduring works. Intellectuals like Wang Yangming challenged rigid orthodoxy with calls for moral self-cultivation and inner clarity.

Eventually, the final blow came not from the Manchus directly but from within. In 1644, the rebel leader Li Zicheng stormed Beijing, and the last Ming emperor took his own life. A desperate Ming general, Wu Sangui, opened the gates of the Great Wall to the Manchus, hoping they could defeat the rebels. They did, but once the Manchus were inside, they never left. They swept through the capital and established a new dynasty, the Qing, which would rule China until the dawn of the 20th century.

Chapter 6: The Qing— China's Last Dynasty

"Your foreign ships come hither, striving the one with the other for our trade, and for the simple reason of their strong desire to reap profit. By what principle of reason, then, should these foreigners send in return a poisonous drug, which involves in destruction those very natives of China?"

-Commissioner Lin Zexu[9]

The ruling line of the Qing dynasty was rooted in the Jurchen people, who were originally semi-nomadic tribes in northeastern China and the founders of the Jin dynasty. By the 15th century, the Jurchens had become Ming tributaries. They regularly sent tribute and received titles and trade privileges. Though still officially vassals to the Ming court, their repeated interactions familiarized them with Chinese bureaucratic and military structures.

When Nurhaci rose to unify the Jianzhou Jurchen tribes, he borrowed strategically from both Ming governance and Mongol organizational methods. He formalized the Eight Banners system, creating a military and administrative framework that became the bedrock of Manchu identity and later Qing rule.

As their ambitions grew, the Manchus expanded their army, and they relied not only on Jurchen warriors but also on defecting Han Chinese

---

[9] Clements, Jonathan. *A Brief History of China*. 2019. Pg. 320.

soldiers. Marriages were brokered between prominent Han officers and Manchu nobility to lock in loyalty. These alliances made it increasingly difficult for the Ming to retain loyalty among their former subjects, even though Ming leaders were slow to fully grasp the emerging threat.

The Manchu rulers treated the Chinese defectors well, valuing the military expertise they brought with them and rewarding them heartily for their contributions. Along with troops, the Manchu also recruited artisans and technicians of all sorts from China and Korea. Due to Manchu largesse, working for the Manchu soon became more appealing than working for the Ming.

In 1625, Nurhaci designated Mukden (now Shenyang) as his capital. He claimed legitimacy that was reminiscent of Chinese emperors by embracing the concept of the Mandate of Heaven. In 1616, he formally established the Later Jin state. By 1636, Nurhaci's successor, Hong Taiji, renamed the people, switching from Jurchen to Manchu, and the realm as Great Qing, cementing his broader ambitions.

Meanwhile, the Ming dynasty, though increasingly pushed southward, still ruled parts of China. While all of these maneuvers by the Manchu were being made, China was facing an economic downturn. The flow of silver from the Americas had dropped off, and market prices in China were affected. Making matters worse was a series of poor harvests due to droughts and other climatic disturbances. Revolts were common in China, and even the military could not be counted on to mount a proper defense of the realm. The Manchu knew as much. In 1644, a Manchu army poured into Beijing and took the Chinese capital without any resistance.

The Chinese emperor, whose army and advisers had abandoned him, took his own life. Even so, the Qing had trouble consolidating their power since various warlords had risen up in pockets that remained out of their reach, such as in deep southwestern China and even on the island of Taiwan.

The Qing invaded Taiwan in 1683 to stamp out the last vestige of Ming power and officially annexed the island. After the annexation of Taiwan, Qing China began to consider expanding its frontiers even further. Expansions were made into Tibet and the southwestern region of what is now called Xinjiang province.

The most effective ruler of the Qing dynasty was the Kangxi Emperor (also referred to as Emperor Shengzu of Qing). He ruled from 1661 to

1722. After China's borders were consolidated under the Kangxi Emperor, he began to reach out to the Chinese diaspora, encouraging trade all throughout Southeast Asia, the Philippines, and other nearby regions. However, as they were looking toward the south, incursions began to occur in their northern frontiers.

These incursions into the reaches of Manchuria were instigated by Russian adventurers seeking land and resources outside of Russia's own known boundaries. They ventured into lands whose exact boundaries had been obscure for centuries. These daring Russians decided to create their own definition of where the Russian border was by building fortresses in the region. This led to direct conflict between the Russian and Qing forces in 1685. Ultimately, the Russians signed the Treaty of Nerchinsk with China in 1689 to settle these border disputes.

When the Kangxi Emperor died in 1722, he was succeeded by his son and heir, who became known as the Yongzheng Emperor. His reign, which lasted until 1735, was much shorter and more troubled than that of his father. During his time on the throne, the Qing attempted to absorb many non-Han groups that had long lived on the periphery of Chinese society. They encouraged Han colonization of frontier regions, co-opted local tribal elites into official roles, and even enforced the Manchu queue hairstyle on Han men as a visible sign of submission. Still, bloody revolts, like the Miao uprisings, made it clear that these efforts were often ham-fisted and poorly received.

After his death in 1735, he was succeeded by a much more successful leader—the Qianlong Emperor. The Qianlong Emperor came to power with an already well-established and efficient bureaucratic system in place, as well as a treasury overflowing with resources. It was up to him to make the most of all this.

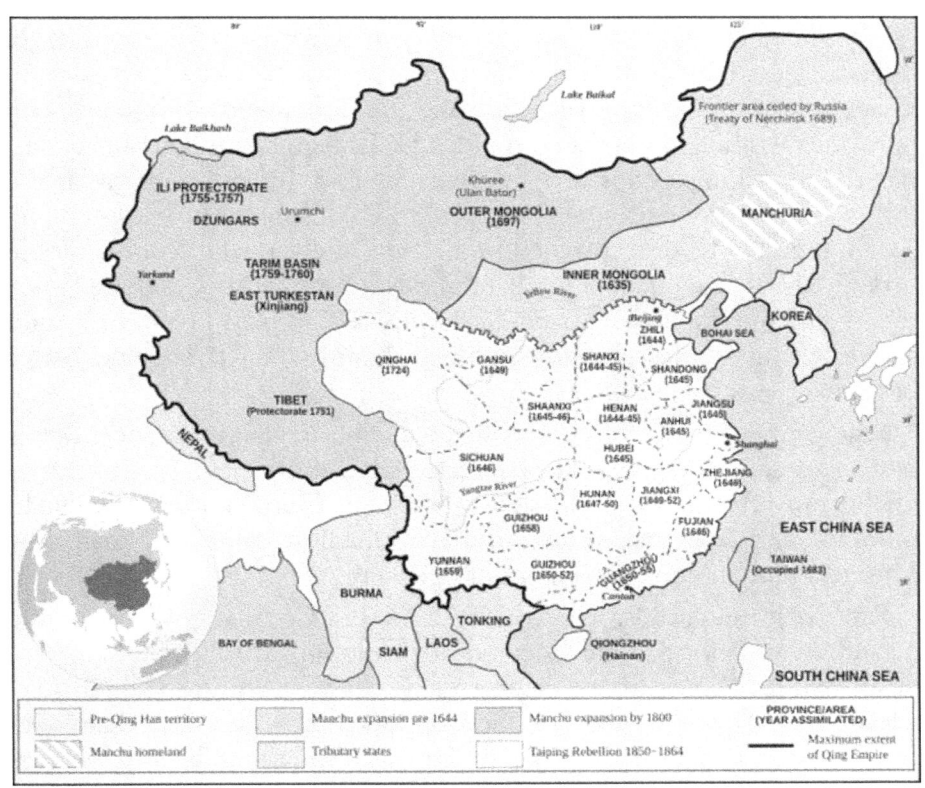

The Qing dynasty around 1820.[15]

The Qing began to allow some quiet outreach to foreign nations. Christian missionaries, in particular, had gained acceptance, with Qing officials viewing the religion as harmless and those who espoused it as peaceful and perhaps even helpful. However, when a dispute arose over ancestor worship among Chinese converts, the emperor began to change his mind. There was a great controversy between Christian missionaries over what it actually meant to revere one's ancestors. Some Christians allowed the traditional practice of ancestor worship, insisting that it was merely a cultural artifact of Chinese society and that it should not impact one's belief in Christianity at all. Others insisted that this form of worshipful reverence was an example of polytheism and came straight from the pits of hell.

The situation came to a head when Pope Clement XI weighed in on the matter and forbade the practice outright. These developments were viewed as rather troubling disturbances by Qing officials and led to a push against Christian missionaries.

This would not put a stop to European inroads in China, though; instead, it would just make Europeans switch gears. Instead of missionaries, the Qing dynasty would be inundated with European merchants wishing to enter into trade. The British, like other Europeans, traded with China exclusively through the East India Company at the port of Canton (modern-day Guangzhou). Under the Canton System, all foreign merchants were confined to this port and forced to conduct trade through licensed Chinese merchant guilds known as the Cohong. They were restricted in their movements, required to pay heavy fees, and dependent on Chinese intermediaries to handle their goods and barter for them.

One of the most prized goods was tea. The British had grown rather fond of tea, and its trade had proved to be a lucrative enterprise. But as much as the British were addicted to tea from China, the British sought to inflict an altogether more virulent addiction on the Chinese by shipping them an enormous amount of opium.

Starting in the 1780s, the British East India Company was operating in tandem with local opium dealers to bring the drug to China. With these secret dealings in the background, on July 25th, 1793, a British delegation led by Ambassador George Macartney famously landed in China to seek greater trade opportunities with the Qing dynasty. George Macartney gained an audience with the Qianlong Emperor and was initially under the impression that his delegation was being well received. But after a while, he came to understand that he was merely being humored and delayed. He realized that his entreaties were being ignored. In October, the Qianlong Emperor made his intentions clear on the subject.

He basically stated that although foreigners, like the British, desired to have unfettered trade with China, the Chinese themselves did not actually need it. On the contrary, the Qianlong Emperor insisted that China had everything it could possibly want within its own borders. Essentially, the emperor was making it seem that it was really the Chinese who were doing the British a favor by allowing trade with them. The British were more or less told that Canton would remain the port through which trade would be conducted and that the status quo of the situation would not change.

Little did the emperor know that the British had been quietly cultivating opium addiction in China. They indeed had something that many Chinese craved. After collecting opium crops in British-controlled

India, the Brits brought shipments of the drug into Canton. An estimated four thousand chests of opium were delivered in 1787. This number steadily increased to an annual amount of some thirty thousand chests by the year 1833.

The Qianlong Emperor abdicated in 1796 in favor of his son, the Jiaqing Emperor, although he continued to wield influence until his death in 1799. The empire was grappling with rising opium addiction. The Jiaqing Emperor found it difficult to manage this growing crisis. He ruled until 1820, when he died of a stroke at the age of fifty-nine. His successor, the Daoguang Emperor, recognized the severity of the opium problem and appointed Lin Zexu as commissioner to combat it.[10]

During the course of Lin Zexu's investigation, he sent a letter to none other than Britain's monarch, Queen Victoria. In this missive to the young queen, who had just taken the throne a few years prior, the Chinese commissioner demanded to know why the British were so intent on shipping harmful narcotics into Chinese ports after China had been—as he described it—so gracious to them. There was a desire to know whether this was just blind greed on the part of British merchants or if there was a larger, more complicated geopolitical strategy at work. To this very day, there is much argument over what the British government was up to. Were they trying to use opium to put a dent in Chinese power?

After writing this letter, Lin Zexu began cracking down on the opium issue. In 1839, he began arresting addicts and dealers. At the beginning of his campaign, the commissioner arrested numerous addicts and local dealers and seized around seventy thousand opium pipes.

Lin Zexu also had a large team of assistants who took it upon themselves to destroy the opium itself, burning it up and dumping its remnants into the ocean. For the commissioner, it was a legal matter; these people were breaking the law by using and selling what the Chinese government considered to be an illegal drug. The recreational smoking of opium had been made illegal in 1729, although opium was allowed for some medicinal purposes. Even so, opium kept coming in by the boatload—literally. In fact, it is said that by the early 1800s, thousands of chests of opium were being shipped to China per year. This opium was shipped into China by foreign vessels that typically would not allow

---

[10] Tanner, Harold. *China: A History From the Great Qing Empire through the People's Republic of China, 1644-2009.* 2010. Pg. 60.

Chinese officials to inspect them. That began to change under the direction of Lin Zexu.[11]

However, when Commissioner Lin Zexu seized massive quantities of British opium in Canton and ordered it publicly destroyed, the British were outraged. Even though the opium was confiscated on Chinese soil, British officials claimed it was a direct assault on their national honor and, more importantly to them, on their profits. The saber-rattling began almost immediately. By November 1839, the First Opium War had officially kicked off, with naval skirmishes breaking out between British warships and Chinese junks near the Chinese coast.

The overall conflict between Britain and China was largely a naval one, with sea battles occurring up and down China's coastline. At one point, the British managed to make their way up the Yangtze River all the way to Nanjing (formerly known as Nanking). This conflict raged until the beaten and battered Chinese sued for peace in 1842.

The resulting peace treaty (the Treaty of Nanking) had the Chinese cough up several supposed treaty ports, with Guangzhou, Xiamen, Fuzhou, Ningbo, and Shanghai being among them. More importantly, the British had been given Hong Kong Island. The British would continue to add to their control of Hong Kong, which they ruled until 1997, when the British government formally ceded control of the city back to China.

Along with all of this, China was forced to pay a huge amount of money for damages. Chinese authorities also received a terrible blow since the treaty forced them to treat British visitors with extra special care. Due to the imposition of extraterritorial measures, any Brit suspected of committing a crime could not be handled by the Chinese justice system. Instead, they were to be placed into the hands of British authorities, who would then subject them to British law rather than Chinese law. This meant that if a visiting sailor harassed Chinese citizens, the best the Chinese government could do to protect its own people was to alert British authorities and hope that the British would deal fairly with the administration of justice.

It was indeed a humiliating thing for the Chinese not to be able to enforce their own laws when visiting foreigners chose to break them. The Chinese had attempted to use their own legal mechanisms to thwart

---

[11] Tanner, Harold. *China: A History From the Great Qing Empire through the People's Republic of China, 1644-2009.* Pg. 75.

the shipment of opium by foreigners. Now, they could not even detain a foreign opium smuggler even if they wanted to. Their hands were most certainly tied.

Another blow to Chinese esteem was that the British insisted that the Chinese give them "Most Favored Nation Status." This meant the British would take on a dominant role in any potential treaties China might make with other actors on the world stage. The situation would grow worse for China as other countries sought their own unequal treaty arrangements.

China was increasingly preyed upon. It was pushed around by foreign powers, and its ability to respond weakened by the year. The pressure finally tipped in 1856 when Qing officials boarded the *Arrow*, a Chinese-owned ship flying the British flag, suspecting piracy. The seizure infuriated the British, who saw it as a blatant affront to their rights and used it as justification for war.

Meanwhile, the Xianfeng Emperor, who had inherited an already collapsing empire in 1850, was losing his grip. While he remained emperor in name, much of the real power slipped from his hands, especially as regional armies and court regents began steering the state through the crisis. The Second Opium War erupted shortly afterward, and amid military defeats and rebellion, the emperor would die in 1861, not long after the court fled Beijing.[12]

During the Second Opium War, troops were sent inland. In December 1857, the British disembarked at Canton and marched all the way to the local governor's home. They seized the governor and sent him packing all the way to British-controlled India. Yes, even though the British insisted on a hands-off policy as it pertained to British citizens, the British brazenly kidnapped a Chinese governor and held him prisoner.

Worse was yet to come. In 1859, the British again sent troops into mainland China, and this time, they marched all the way to Beijing. Here, they set fire to the famed Summer Palace, burning it to the ground. The Chinese were in a state of shock and ultimately capitulated to demands. They signed a brand new treaty on October 24th, 1860.

---

[12] Tanner, Harold. *China: A History From the Great Qing Empire through the People's Republic of China, 1644-2009.* Pg. 87.

The Summer Palace.[16]

This treaty led to more territorial concessions from China, giving the British control of the Kowloon Peninsula. It also had China paying out more money in addition to the indemnities that were already being paid. China was forced to allow Christian missionaries to freely preach in China, something it had previously resisted. But even though Chinese officials were being forced to agree to such draconian terms, that did not mean the large population of China itself was going to agree and be on the same page.

Well before the treaty was inked, China was already convulsed by one of its deadliest upheavals in history: the Taiping Rebellion. This popular revolt had political and quasi-religious overtones. At the heart of this uprising was a local rebel leader (and a shaman of sorts) named Hong Xiuquan.

Hong came from a rather obscure background. As a young adult, he had failed the civil service exams and subsequently had a nervous breakdown. He then began to have visions (some might say hallucinations), in which he saw a man with a white beard, extolling him to pick up his sword and battle against the forces of darkness. He also saw a younger man, whom he believed to be the old man's son.

Initially, Hong did not understand what he was seeing, but after reading a Christian tract, he had an epiphany. He came to believe that the old man was God and that the young man was none other than

God's only begotten son, Jesus Christ. This was not the end of Hong's revelations, though. He soon came to believe that he was also a son of God, making him Christ's own brother.

Hong pored over the scriptures and decided that he was picking up where Jesus had left off. Similar to how Jesus remarked that the "Kingdom of Heaven was at hand," Hong began to proclaim that he was destined to usher in this heavenly kingdom and that the heart of this kingdom would be located right inside China itself.

Hong had a lot of followers, especially among poor farmers and those who felt abandoned by the Qing government. But China—then as now—was vast and diverse, and not everyone was buying what Hong was selling. Faced with opposition and unwillingness to convert, Hong decided that persuasion alone was not going to cut it. He raised a massive rebel army, and in 1853, they stormed Nanjing, capturing it and declaring it the capital of their so-called Heavenly Kingdom. A couple of years later, in 1855, he and his forces laid siege to Beijing. The rebels were pushed back at this point, but the preoccupied Qing government was not able to stamp out the rebellion completely. The rebels holed up in their stronghold in Nanjing, where they continued to defy the Qing.

A scene of the Taiping Rebellion.[17]

In January 1864, the armies of the Qing managed to surround the bulk of the Taiping military in Nanjing. The Qing forces had their foes right where they wanted them, and they laid siege to the city. Hong perished in the struggle. His followers were likely disheartened after his death, which led to the fall of the city. By June, the Qing were in full control of the Kingdom of Heaven's capital.[13]

---

[13] Tanner, Harold. *China: A History From the Great Qing Empire through the People's Republic of China, 1644-2009.* Pg. 88.

Although the Qing defeated the rebels, the fact that they had held out for so long showed just how difficult a time the Qing were having. They faced multiple outside threats and internal discord, so they had to put out many fires on different fronts.

There were still problems to deal with, especially when a resurgent Japan came to take its piece of the Chinese pie. Japan had watched very closely what was happening in China, and its people were determined not to have it replicated in Japanese territory.

In 1868, in an effort to rapidly modernize, Japan kicked off the Meiji Restoration, which was named after the ambitious Japanese Emperor Meiji. While China had failed to modernize due to the lack of an industrial base and isolationist policies, Japan was astonishingly successful in its efforts. In a feverish rush of activity akin to the Manhattan Project or the moon landing, Japan pulled all of its resources and manpower into a tremendous national effort. The country managed to make rapid advancements that would have taken other countries decades (if not centuries) in just a few years.

Japan developed a strong industrial base and began pumping out modern armaments. These armaments were sent aboard brand-new Japanese naval craft, allowing the military to begin to make inroads against the staggering and failing power of China. This aggressive posturing came to a head in 1894 when Japan invaded Korea.

This was not the first time Japan had tried its luck at invading Korea. You may recall that Japan had launched an invasion of Korea during the Ming dynasty. It took a considerable amount of resources to push the Japanese out, and it is believed the invasion contributed to the weakening of the Ming dynasty, eventually allowing the Manchu to take over and establish the Qing dynasty. Yes, the Ming had repelled the Japanese at great cost, but the Qing would not be so lucky.

This second historic invasion of Korea by Japan was a clear bit of aggression on Japan's part, but it was not merely motivated by conquest (although that was certainly a part of it). Many Japanese military advisers viewed the taking of Korea as a preemptive defensive measure to better safeguard Japan itself. At its closest point, Korea lies just 120 miles from Japan. The Japanese feared that if China fell to the Europeans, Korea would soon be occupied by them as well. If Korea had become a European colony, it would not have been too hard to launch an invasion from Korea against Japan. The Japanese basically reasoned that if China could not protect Korea, then they would go in and take control of it for themselves.

When the Korean government was threatened by an internal coup attempt, it asked the Chinese for military assistance. However, the Japanese inserted themselves into the picture. It was not long before Japanese and Chinese troops came to blows. The fighting over Korea, which ultimately became known as the First Sino-Japanese War, erupted in July 1894.

During this conflict, the Japanese, despite their much smaller numbers, managed to deal China stunning defeats in battle after battle. The Japanese demonstrated that they had a much keener grasp of advanced military equipment and methods. In an incredible reversal, mighty China actually had to bow down to Japan. In the subsequent treaty China made with the victor, the Chinese agreed to give up Taiwan and relinquish all claims on Korea. Japan would slowly sink its teeth into Korea, first proclaiming it as a Japanese protectorate before annexing the territory completely in 1910.

China's embarrassing defeat in the First Sino-Japanese War sparked a wave of resentment and unrest among the Chinese masses. That bitterness simmered for years until it boiled over in 1900. In northern China, the martial societies known as the "Boxers" rose in a violent campaign against missionaries, foreign legations, and the Qing's foreign entanglements.

Similar to the Taiping Rebellion, the Boxer Rebellion was a revolt with religious overtones. The Boxers were called as such because they were martial artists who knew how to use their fists. This skill was apparently on full display when they made their way into Beijing in 1900 and began randomly assaulting the foreigners they found there.

The Boxers seem to have especially had it out for foreign missionaries. They feared that the foreign missionaries were spies and saw them as instigators. The Boxers also resented the fact that they would often intervene in legal matters between Christian Chinese and non-Christian Chinese residents.[14]

As a massive horde of angry ruffians descended upon them in Beijing, foreigners were forced to seek refuge in and around foreign embassies.

---

[14] Tanner, Harold. *China: A History From the Great Qing Empire through the People's Republic of China, 1644-2009.* Pg. 97.

Chinese Christians were also forced to flee, as their churches were burned and people were assaulted. It is believed that thousands of Chinese Christians were forced to leave to avoid the violence of the Boxers.

This tumult certainly did not go unnoticed. It soon got the attention of foreign power brokers and a coalition of European states, as well as Japan. A multinational force, said to have been around twenty thousand strong, was sent in to put down the revolt.

Even though the Chinese government claimed the uprising was spontaneous in nature, the current Qing ruler, Empress Dowager Cixi, was still held accountable. Upon the threat of further military intervention, she was forced to sign the Boxer Protocol. Under these stipulations, China was forced to allow the stationing of foreign troops in Beijing and was forced to pay a hefty fee in reparations. Furthermore, any Chinese organization deemed to have even a hint of anti-foreigner sentiment was officially banned under penalty of execution. In doing so, Empress Dowager Cixi signed what could be called a death warrant for both her regime and herself. The crushing terms of the Boxer Protocol stripped the Qing of what little autonomy it had left, and the dynasty was never the same again. She died on November 15th, 1908, officially from dysentery—or perhaps a complication of pneumonia—but rumors of foul play lingered for decades.

However, if outside powers thought that coming down hard on the Qing dynasty would bring order to China, they were gravely mistaken. This latest crackdown only led to even more discontent among the Chinese.

Up until this point, many of the rebellions that broke out were supposedly done in the name of the Qing. The Boxers claimed they were trying to restore China's prestige on behalf of the Qing dynasty, which was why their attacks were on foreigners, not on Qing officials. According to scholar and historian Jonathan Clements, the slogan shouted by the Boxers was "Support the Qing, expel the foreigners."[15]

In the aftermath of the failed Boxer uprising, the rebels seemed to have a change of heart. It was realized that the only way to bring China back to its glory days was to topple the Qing government itself. From this

---

[15] Clements, Jonathan. *A Brief History of China*. Pg. 330.

point forward, the attacks were not so much on outsiders as they were on Qing insiders.

Around this time, a young Chinese woman named Qiu Jin came to prominence. Born in 1875, Qiu Jin came of age during the Boxer Rebellion. She went on to marry and have two children, but the traditional life of a Chinese housewife just did not satisfy her. She wanted more. Qui Jin ended up leaving her husband and children (something highly unusual for the time) and traveling to Japan, where she studied abroad.

Befriending local intelligentsia, she learned about philosophy and all manner of political and social theories. She then returned to China in 1905 and became actively involved in anti-Qing revolts. Along with being a rabble-rouser, Qui Jin was known as a great writer. She could stir even the hardest of hearts with her stirring poetic prose. Many of her poems and other writings could be found in a magazine-style periodical, for which she served as the editor.

Qui Jin was not only a champion of overthrowing the Qing dynasty; she was also an advocate for women's rights. She condemned the practice of foot binding, which was still widespread. Foot binding is the practice of binding up the feet of Chinese girls so that their feet will be small. However, their feet would also be deformed as a result.

Qiu Jin drew a direct parallel between the practice of foot binding and the constant social binding of women. Even though foot binding was an obvious means of physically crippling Chinese women so they could obtain "desirable" feet, the oppressive, male-dominated Chinese society had other methods at its disposal to keep women confined. Girls were routinely denied an education; they were kept deliberately illiterate so they would not get any ideas about independence. Most women were forced into arranged marriages and treated as bargaining chips in family deals, with no say in the matter. Once married, they had little to no legal rights. They were unable to own property, initiate divorce, or move freely. Their lives were expected to play out in the shadows, behind doors, and far from the public eye. Even in widowhood, they were chained to outdated ideals. They were expected to remain chaste for the rest of their lives, even if it meant a lifetime alone. In Qiu Jin's eyes, all of this was just another kind of binding—and she was determined to cut the cords.

Qui Jin was most certainly a progressive for the period, and she believed that obtaining full and equal rights for all Chinese was the only possible path forward. She was known for her eccentric (at least eccentric by early 1900s standards) habit of dressing like a man, not wearing makeup, and riding around on a horse, with a Japanese sword dangling at her side. She definitely stood out from the crowd and was rather hard to miss. But she also never made any attempt to hide.

Along with being a writer and editor, she also ran a girls' school called the Datong School for Girls. However, the school also served as a front for the instruction of Chinese republican radicals who were hellbent on overthrowing the Qing government and installing a Chinese republic in its place. Once these activities were uncovered, the heavy hand of the Qing came down on the Datong School and ultimately Qui Jin herself. She could hardly deny being involved since she was nursing a badly hurt hand when the authorities arrived. She had been injured in a failed attempt to make a bomb. Her own cousin had also been recently implicated in an attack on the police.

Her friends had received word of the crackdown ahead of time and tried to warn Qui to flee. Qui Jin was adamant in her refusal to do so. She insisted that instead of running from the Qing officials she had been harrying, she was going to stand her ground. It is unclear what she hoped to achieve besides becoming a martyr for the cause, but she insisted that she would stay.

Qui Jin stayed inside while soldiers surrounded the compound and engaged in gunfights with the students and rebels outside. The troops then went in and grabbed Qui Jin, dragging her out into the street. She was then brought to the local station, where she was brutally interrogated. She refused to confess to any crimes, so a confession was written for her. Her torturers then asked her to sign it. She refused. Supposedly, she wrote the words to one last poem instead. She was then sentenced to death.

She was convicted without a trial and without a jury. The sentence was carried out a short time later. In 1907, Qui Jin had her head chopped off in a public square known as Xuanting Crossing. She became a martyr for the revolution. She did not live to see the events play out, but it all happened in rather rapid-fire fashion after her death. In the following year, 1908, Empress Dowager Cixi perished. She left the throne to her two-year-old nephew, who became the Xuantong Emperor.

Of course, the infant would have advisers rule in his stead, but despite any best intentions, a renewed reign of Qing authority was simply not to be. In 1911, the Qing dynasty collapsed under its own ineffectual weight. Many rebel factions had made this collapse possible, but a radical revolutionary by the name of Sun Yat-sen had risen to particular prominence.

Sun Yat-sen had trained as a physician in his youth and often applied his diagnostic instincts to the deeper ailments of Chinese society. He concluded that it was the outdated thinking and oppressive structures of the monarchy that were poisoning the body politic. Driven by that insight, he became a radical revolutionary determined to overthrow the Qing dynasty.

A colorized photograph of Sun Yat-sen.[18]

His zeal got him into serious trouble. Forced into exile, Sun Yat-sen ended up in London. In October 1896, he was detained at the Chinese legation for over a week. The legation attempted to send him back to Beijing for execution, but thanks to the intervention of sympathetic British allies and mounting public outcry, Sun was released. The incident gave him international fame and further legitimacy as a revolutionary leader.[16]

Back in China, the Qing monarchy was on its last legs. The Guangxu Emperor, who had once shown promise as a reformer, died under mysterious circumstances while under house arrest. Empress Dowager Cixi, who was still the power behind the throne, named her infant nephew Puyi as emperor. But with Puyi too young to rule, power passed to a series of ineffective regents. Within just a few years, the entire imperial system collapsed. In 1912, Puyi abdicated, bringing more than two thousand years of dynastic rule in China to an end.[17]

---

[16] Tanner, Harold. *China: A History From the Great Qing Empire through the People's Republic of China, 1644-2009.* Pg. 96.

[17] Tanner, Harold. *China: A History From the Great Qing Empire through the*

Although Sun Yat-sen was a big player in all of this, he ultimately deferred authority to Yuan Shikai, a fellow revolutionary and former military general. Sun Yat-sen saw to it that Yuan became the provisional president for what he hoped would be a Chinese republic. However, Yuan became a bit power-mad, and in 1915, he actually tried to make himself emperor for life.

Yuan Shikai.[19]

The other factions within the movement quickly turned against Yuan when they found out, and they pulled the plug on his ambitious pretensions. Yuan's attempt was thwarted, but China was thrown into chaos once again, with various factions fighting each other.

The world was changing in the meantime. World War I had erupted, and in the midst of all that, a massive communist revolution erupted in Russia in 1917, laying the foundations for the Soviet Union. This ideology quickly spread to China, and in 1921, China's Communist Party first took shape.

People's Republic of China, 1644-2009. Pg. 117.

Sun Yat-sen passed his authority to a powerful general named Chiang Kai-shek, who was able to gain dominance over the other warring factions of the revolution. By 1929, Chiang Kai-shek seemingly had a solid grip on the country, as well as a powerful base in the capital city of Nanjing (Nanking).

However, the Communists were growing underground and out of sight under the leadership of Mao Zedong. Mao Zedong began his career as a young radical and steadily rose through the ranks. The Communists would emerge in force in 1931 after a Chinese Soviet Republic was declared. This base lasted for a few years before it was dismantled by Chiang Kai-shek and his Nationalist army.

Mao Zedong—whatever his faults—was a shrewd and cunning military strategist. He knew that the Communists were not yet ready to face the might of the Nationalist army head-on. So, instead, he perfected a form of highly effective guerrilla warfare. He and his army hid just out of reach of the Nationalists. He directed his forces to only engage in quick surgical strikes against specific targets before melting back into the wilderness. This strategy whittled down the fighting capacity of the Nationalists, and the Communists were able to minimize their losses.

The struggle between these two camps would be interrupted and effectively put on hold when Japan once again made aggressive inroads in China. The Japanese, who had already seized Korea, decided to seize the neighboring region of northeastern China, otherwise known as Manchuria. The Japanese engineered a regime change by installing Manchu leadership and branding the puppet state of Manchukuo as a newly resurrected Manchu realm. They installed the exiled former emperor Puyi as ruler in a political move meant to legitimize their control. The audacity of creating a revived monarchy under Japanese direction alarmed both the Nationalists and the Communists. In the face of this foreign imposition, they agreed to a fragile, temporary truce. They put aside their civil war and united, at least in name, to resist Japanese aggression.

Chapter 7: World War II and China's Civil War

"The superior man, when resting in safety, does not forget that danger may come."

-Confucius[18]

China's renewed problems with Japan first erupted in 1931 during the Mukden incident. The Mukden incident occurred in the Japanese-controlled region of Manchuria. Although the incident is still shrouded in some obscurity, most scholars believe the Japanese sabotaged their own railroad tracks and then turned around and blamed the Chinese for it.

The Japanese used this as a reason to forcibly occupy the region and ultimately transform it into a Japanese-controlled puppet state, which they referred to as Manchukuo. The Japanese were creeping steadily closer to the Chinese heartland, as they now controlled Korea and the bordering region of Manchuria. From 1932 to 1935, they would seize more territory in Inner Mongolia and make aggressive advances toward the Shanxi, Shandong, and Suiyuan regions.

Chiang Kai-shek's Nationalist government mostly ignored this aggression, feeling as if the bigger threat to Chinese society was the Communists inside China. Mao Zedong and his band were forced into

---

[18] Brewer, D. *Quotes of Confucius and Their Interpretations: A Words of Wisdom Collection Book.* Pg. 45.

hiding. They embarked upon the "Long March" into the remote reaches of China from October 1934 to October 1935. This retreat from Chiang Kai-shek's Nationalist troops would have the Communists trekking some six thousand miles. They marched from Jiangxi, located in China's southeast, all the way to Shaanxi province in the north.[19]

This sentiment would change on July 7th, 1937. Ever since the Boxer Protocol, China had been forced to allow nations, including Japan, which had legates in Beijing, to have their own military guard to serve as protection. This was due to the fact that the Boxers had attacked foreigners, and the Chinese government had seemed unable or unwilling to protect them. It was for this reason that the Japanese had troops on the Marco Polo Bridge in the first place.

The Marco Polo Bridge incident occurred when a Japanese soldier did not return to his post. The Japanese insisted on being able to send in troops to look for the missing man. The Chinese refused, which led to a tense stand-off that ultimately resulted in the exchange of gunfire. This incident spiraled into the Second Sino-Japanese War. Just a couple of years later, this war would become a theater of conflict in the larger conflagration of World War II. In fact, the Marco Polo Bridge incident could be considered the starting point of World War II, although historians generally cite Germany's 1939 invasion of Poland as the start of the war.

In 1940, Japan entered into an alliance with fellow fascist belligerents, Germany and Italy. They would battle the Allied forces, which were led by the United States, Britain, the Soviet Union, and, ultimately, China.

After the Marco Polo Bridge incident, the fighting continued to escalate. By December of 1937, Japanese troops were storming into Nanjing, which led to the infamous "Rape of Nanking." It is believed that the Japanese killed hundreds of thousands of Chinese, many of them civilians.

The use of the word "rape" is not an exaggeration either since the Japanese routinely used rape as a weapon of war and retribution. The city of Nanjing saw some of the worst depredations in recorded history. Japanese troops stormed into homes. They murdered husbands, fathers, and sons, and then they had their way with the women living there.

---

[19] Tanner, Harold. *China: A History From the Great Qing Empire through the People's Republic of China, 1644-2009.* Pg. 163.

Captured Chinese captives. It is believed that all of them were killed within days.[30]

Before the year 1937 was through, Nanjing had been decimated, and other major Chinese cities had likewise fallen in quick succession. Shanghai fell to the Japanese, as did Guangzhou. The Japanese ended up dominating northern China and set up their own capital in Nanjing. The Chinese government was forced to move farther south and regroup in Sichuan province.

Despite suffering devastating losses, the Chinese army was still intact and could tap a large pool of manpower. Although Sichuan province had its fair share of resources, China's main industrial capacity was in the northeastern cities that Japan had taken over. The Chinese forces had also lost access to important ports that were crucial for the importation of war materiel.

Even so, the Chinese resistance refused to give up and would remain a stubborn thorn in Japan's side. This led to even more brutal tactics. The Japanese air force began a ruthless bombing campaign, hoping to shock the Chinese resistance into submission. The Japanese also tried their hand at propaganda to bring the Chinese populace on their side.

In 1940, the Japanese took things a step further by installing a puppet ruler, Wang Jingwei, a former political rival of Chiang Kai-shek who had turned collaborator. Stationed in Nanjing, Wang led what was called the Reorganized National Government of China. While this move gave the appearance of legitimacy, it was widely dismissed across China. The memories of Japanese atrocities, particularly the horrors of Nanjing, were still fresh. Even those who might have once sympathized with Wang were unlikely to lend him their support under such circumstances.

Demonstrating a strong sense of patriotism (whether they supported the Communist or Nationalist factions), the Chinese citizens rose up in solidarity against the Japanese. Japanese-controlled areas became depopulated as Chinese fled south and west to more distant reaches where they would be free from the grasp of their aggressors. These Chinese refugees joined the armed struggle or provided much-needed manpower to build up infrastructure in the new bases of resistance.

Although the Nationalists and the Communists were ostensibly working together to push back the Japanese, Chiang Kai-shek and Mao Zedong quietly consolidated their own bases of power, preparing for an inevitable new round of fighting between them as soon as the Japanese were defeated.

During the war, Chiang Kai-shek, as leader of the Nationalists, was the public face of China. He was the officially recognized leader of the Chinese, and the Allied powers dealt with him. Mao Zedong was an underground leader during this period. It is likely no one ever dreamed that he would eventually rise up to become China's supreme leader.

By 1942, the Japanese were already in retreat. Japan had made the mistake of bombing Pearl Harbor, Hawaii, which brought the United States into the war. After the Battle of Midway, which took place in early June 1942, Japan was steadily being pushed back on all fronts. The Japanese were ultimately defeated in the summer of 1945.

Mao Zedong had been consolidating his grip on the CCP (the Chinese Communist Party). Shortly after the war had come to a close, a referendum was held in which Mao was made chairman of the party. Right on the heels of Mao being made chairman, Chiang Kai-shek extended an invitation to Mao to speak with him.

Mao met Chiang at the Nationalist stronghold in Chongqing in Sichuan province. The meeting received worldwide attention, with the international press widely covering the event. The two men seemed to be in good spirits as they drank and spoke with one another. They likely had a lot to reminisce about, whether they were swapping war stories about the Japanese or even accounts of run-ins that their mutual armed forces had with each other.

The most encouraging thing for witnesses to the talks was simply the fact that these two were *talking*. For one brief moment, it seemed that perhaps the two factions of China could come together and that some sort of compromise might be made in order to avoid civil war. However, such things were not meant to be. Despite the nice talk the two had with each other, it was only a short time later that the previously stalled conflict between the Nationalists and the Communists reignited.

It was a long, bitter struggle, but the Communists eventually gained the upper hand. The Nationalists were ultimately pushed right off the mainland of China and forced to evacuate to the island of Taiwan. The Japanese, who had previously controlled Taiwan, had already left, leaving a power vacuum in their absence.

China entered the postwar era deeply unsettled but with a flicker of promise. The Cairo Declaration of November 1943 committed the Allies to restore both Taiwan and Manchuria to Chinese control, specifically to the Nationalist Republic of China under Chiang Kai-shek, not Mao's Communists. This guarantee still fuels today's Taiwan question.

After Japan's surrender, Chiang was designated China's postwar leader, but Beijing's recognition could not translate into instant control. In Manchuria, as Japanese forces withdrew, Communist troops under Lin Biao and Zhu De surged northward, seizing Soviet-captured armaments, recruiting former Manchukuo soldiers, and establishing bases in rail-hub and industrial zones. They even disrupted arrival routes for Nationalist reinforcements by destroying rail lines and controlling key ports.

By late 1945, Chiang's forces—though recognized internationally—had only advanced to Mukden (today's Shenyang) and parts of southern China. Meanwhile, the Communists dominated much of the northeast and sizable territories across northern China. The country was effectively carved into two competing spheres: the Communist-held north and the Nationalist south.

A split as deep as this could easily have become permanent; just look at North and South Korea or Vietnam. Yet history ran a different course. As the civil war resumed and the Communists steadily advanced, the Nationalists faltered. By 1949, Chiang and his followers were driven off the mainland, fleeing to Taiwan. Mao proclaimed the People's Republic of China, while Taiwan continued under the Republic of China, a status the island maintains to this day.

It took just a few years after Japan's surrender in 1945 for the Communist faction in China to triumph over the Nationalists. From the fall of the Qing dynasty through Japanese invasion and the subsequent civil war, China had been through quite a bit. However, China's struggle for survival and identity was far from over.

Chapter 8: Red China Rising

"For many years, we Communists have struggled for a cultural revolution as well as for a political and economic revolution, and our aim is to build a new society and a new state for the Chinese nation. That new society and new state will have not only a new politics and a new economy but a new culture."

-Mao Zedong[20]

The communist People's Republic of China was declared on the mainland on October 1st, 1949. The communist Chinese turned inward to figure out just what kind of government and society they were going to form.

Mao and his comrades had some rather lofty ideals that they wanted to fulfill. They wanted to absolutely transform the lives of the average Chinese citizen. They also wanted to fulfill many of the same ambitions that those who rebelled against the Qing in the early 1900s had sought. They wanted a strong, independent nation that was not beholden to the interests of outside forces. They wanted to establish a nation that they could all be proud of, one that would not be kicked around by outside nations. Mao and his followers also wanted to become a wealthy country that had respect on the world stage and a strong army. These were essentially the same ambitions of the very Nationalists the Communists had defeated. However, the Nationalists and Communists differed significantly in how society should be run. The Nationalists sought

---

[20] Clements, Jonathan. *A Brief History of China*. Pg. 348.

democratic freedom (even though it was not always implemented in the early days) for the average person, while the Communists were steadfast in their Marxist ideology, which called for government controls on just about every aspect of Chinese life.

After seizing control of mainland China in 1949, the Communist leadership found itself in uncharted waters. Most of its senior figures had been guerrilla fighters, not administrators, and running one of the world's largest nations was a different kind of battle. Their first priority was the countryside—the heartland of their revolution. They pushed through sweeping land reforms, broke up the holdings of wealthy landlords, and redistributed them to the peasants who had long backed the Communist cause.

Once their grip on power was secure, the focus shifted. By the mid-1950s, Beijing began looking beyond the rice paddies and toward the cities. Industrial growth, centralized planning, and urban infrastructure now became the priorities. This transition was not without friction since policies designed for rural China often clashed with the realities of urban life, but it marked the beginning of the state's long push to modernize China's cities as well as its countryside.

Mao Zedong, in the meantime, began to speak of his desire to create a solid socialist enclave within China and then project that ideology onto the world stage. According to Communists, this meant that cities needed to stop being consumers of goods and become producers of goods. In this struggle for production dominance, he advised that there would have to be a class struggle in order to bring these aims to fruition. The leadership of China would be a dictatorship, but it would be a *people's dictatorship*. The average citizen might not have fully understood all of these new terms. They were weary of decades of war. Most Chinese simply wanted a return to some sort of civilized society. As such, many complied and did their best to follow the communist state's new decrees. Communist-backed police and military units were created and helped greatly in the establishment of order, especially as it pertained to putting a stop to roving bandits, which had become prevalent due to the previous chaos.

China was trying to turn inward at this stage in its development so that it could focus on rebuilding and restructuring its society. But no matter how much China desired to turn its attention to internal affairs, the world stage would soon come calling again in the form of the Korean War.

In the summer of 1950, communist forces from North Korea stormed across the 38th parallel into South Korea. After gaining authorization from the United Nations to intervene, the United States led the charge to drive the North Koreans back. The Soviet Union came out in support of North Korea, as did China.

The Chinese would become directly involved in the war by secretly (at least at first) deploying their own troops into North Korea to take on the American, South Korean, and other allied fighters. An estimated 250,000 Chinese troops were sent to fight alongside the North Koreans. The war was a bloody one, but the United States and its allies managed to push the North Koreans back.

Ultimately, the war ended in an armistice in July 1953. The boundary between North and South Korea was once again the 38th parallel, and the area was established as a demilitarized zone (DMZ). Yes, after all of that bloodshed, the participants in this carnage were right back where they had started.

Right around the time of the Korean War, China also intervened in Tibet. China had long considered Tibet its own territory despite Tibet's history of independence. Tibet had enjoyed de facto independence ever since the fall of the Qing dynasty, but after the Communists consolidated their power in 1949, they started to look toward reestablishing Chinese authority over the Tibetans.

The Chinese launched an invasion of Tibet in 1950. Interestingly, although China's actions were considered an invasion from an outside perspective, the Chinese have always referred to this incident as the peaceful liberation of Tibet. Perspective, of course, is everything, but when Chinese troops came crashing across Tibet's borders on October 7th, 1950, the local Tibetans likely did not see anything all that peaceful or liberating about it. The world was quite distracted by the Korean War at the time, so very little attention was paid to what China was doing in Tibet.

Besides the forced takeover of Tibetan land, the most significant consequence of this action was the displacement of Tibet's religious and political leader, the Dalai Lama. After China's takeover of Tibet, the Dalai Lama was eventually driven into exile. He is still in exile to this day.

Tibet might have been forced to toe the Communist line, but Mao Zedong did not always present himself as an unbending autocrat. In 1956, he launched what became known as the Hundred Flowers

Campaign, urging citizens to "let a hundred flowers bloom, let a hundred schools of thought contend." It was billed as an invitation for open debate, where intellectuals, workers, and officials alike could voice their concerns about the state and its leadership. For a brief moment, criticisms poured in.

By mid-1957, the mood changed abruptly. Mao declared that those outspoken critics were "rightists" seeking to undermine socialism. The campaign gave way to the Anti-Rightist Movement, and thousands of those who had spoken up were purged from their jobs, sent to labor camps, or imprisoned. Whether Mao had planned this reversal from the start or simply decided to turn the campaign into a purge once the criticism cut too deep remains debated, but the result was the same.

In 1958, Mao Zedong embarked upon his Great Leap Forward. This was an ambitious but ill-fated plan to rapidly speed up the industrialization of China. Mao sought to utilize the massive manpower available in China so he could bypass the need for heavy infrastructure.

Mao tried to mitigate the lack of large industrial factories by establishing backyard steel furnaces in local villages. Making matters worse, the technicians tapped to run these clumsy, improvised furnaces were often selected not for their merit or actual skill set and ability to forge steel but because of their adherence to communist ideology. Needless to say, the steel forged by these backyard furnaces was of horrendous quality. Even worse, orders were issued to strip all existing infrastructure of as much steel as possible so that it could be melted into more useful things.

All this accomplished was the destruction of much of China's usable steel. Good-quality tools, machinery, and structural supports were hauled off to be melted in crude backyard furnaces, only to emerge as brittle, worthless lumps of pig iron. These makeshift foundries devoured vast amounts of coal and lumber—the very fuels needed for industry and daily life—just to keep their fires burning.

Along with ineffective (and bizarre) attempts to industrialize China, the Great Leap Forward also sponsored agricultural reform. This also led to disaster. Collective farms were created, and strict quotas were established. It soon became common practice to lie about crop yields just to get a pat on the back from the Communist taskmasters. This led the government to think that they were achieving a bountiful harvest when the yields were actually quite dismal.

Matters became even worse. Mao Zedong, convinced that sparrows were harming grain production, ordered a nationwide campaign to eradicate them. As anyone with a basic grasp of ecosystems could have predicted, this was an ecological catastrophe in the making. Once the sparrow population plummeted, the insects they once kept in check, especially grain-devouring locusts, multiplied in swarms. With no natural predators left to control them, the locusts descended on fields across China, stripping crops bare. This, combined with other agricultural missteps of the Great Leap Forward, helped trigger a famine that raged until 1961.

A moratorium was finally placed on the Great Leap Forward the following year, in 1962. Ultimately, the Great Leap Forward can be summarized as a massive amount of investment, time, and energy that yielded very little. In fact, it did much more damage than it did any good.

This was not only evidenced by the starving and dying people of China but also by economic figures. Rather than propel China forward, the Great Leap Forward, which lasted from 1958 to 1962, saw the Chinese economy shrink.

Interestingly, although the funds were drying up, China still pulled together enough resources to establish itself as a nuclear power. In 1964, in the remote desert of Lop Nur, the Chinese successfully detonated their first atomic bomb—an achievement that shocked the rest of the world. It was codenamed Project 596, and it made China the fifth country on the planet with nuclear capability. Even more remarkable was that they had done it largely on their own. The Soviets had pulled out their scientists and blueprints in the late 1950s during the Sino-Soviet split. For Mao, the test was proof that China could stand shoulder to shoulder with the world's great powers, even though the country was still reeling from economic hardship.

And they weren't done yet. Less than three years later, in 1967, China stunned observers again by testing its first hydrogen bomb, leaping from atomic to thermonuclear status in record time. For a nation still struggling to feed itself, the message was unmistakable: China might be poor, but it was not to be underestimated.

Nevertheless, it was clear that something was deeply wrong with the communist system, China's leadership, or both. Tension and suspicion hung in the air. Out of this volatile climate came what would be called the Cultural Revolution. This was an all-out campaign to root out anyone deemed disloyal to communist ideals. It was nothing short of a reign of terror. The Cultural Revolution was driven by Mao Zedong's infamous Red Guards, who took it upon themselves to expose, humiliate, and often destroy perceived enemies of the revolution.

The Red Guards were a radical mass movement made up largely of indoctrinated youth. Mao understood that young people, with their impulsive energy and uncompromising idealism, were far more likely to throw themselves into the revolution with ferocity. They became his shock troops, carrying out vicious campaigns against anyone suspected of straying from the state's rigid communist orthodoxy.

This led to terrible scenes of students denouncing teachers, children denouncing parents, tenants evicting landlords, and random people on the street having the Red Guards haul them in for questioning. In particular, the Red Guards were seeking out those who were guilty of indulging in what was referred to as the Four Olds: old thinking, old culture, old customs, and old habits.

Mao Zedong's Cultural Revolution felt like it only came to an end when Red Guards overran much of Beijing, storming into the Forbidden City's backyard, only to be checked by armed resistance at the gates. But that was not the end of the chaos. By early 1968, the People's Liberation Army (the army of the People's Republic of China) was forcibly suppressing wild Red Guard factions across major urban centers. Later that year, Mao issued the order that sent most young radicals off to remote farms and rural provinces to be reeducated—a strategy that allowed the state to regain control.

The human cost was staggering. The estimates of those killed during the period range from one to two million, with some accounts suggesting even higher figures. Tens of millions more were persecuted, exiled, or displaced, including the sweeping Down to the Countryside Movement, which uprooted more than ten million urban youth. Entire families were torn apart. Intellectuals, suspected capitalists, and "class enemies" were purged in brutal mass campaigns.

Some of the worst atrocities occurred during mass killings and massacres, such as in Dao County, where over 7,600 were killed or forced to take their own lives. In 1970, the Chinese Communist Party even launched what was called the "One Strike-Three Antis Campaign," targeting supposed counterrevolutionaries, profiteers, and corrupt officials. Nearly 1.9 million people were labeled enemies, with hundreds of thousands arrested or executed, all in the name of ideological cleansing. This horror only truly wound down with Mao's death in 1976 and the arrest of the Gang of Four.

In many ways, the Cultural Revolution could be seen as Mao creating internal enemies for frustrated citizens to attack. This served as a release valve so they could vent their frustration. He likely figured it was better for them to vent their frustration on each other than to turn their wrath on him and his own failed policies.

In the meantime, China was going through external changes as well. Most notably, in July 1971, entreaties were made to the United States by way of President Richard Nixon's adviser, Henry Kissinger, and Mao's top fixer, Zhou Enlai. These two arranged for Nixon and Mao to meet with each other in the spring of 1972. The visit was a political coup for both Nixon and Mao and resulted in one of the most thought-provoking moments of the Cold War.

By this point, the Chinese had experienced a falling-out of sorts with their old benefactor, the Soviet Union. To describe it as a "falling-out" is putting it rather mildly, considering that border skirmishes had actually erupted between the two in 1969.

Mao had begun to fear the Soviet Union more than he ever admired it. He had watched with alarm during the Soviet invasion and occupation of Czechoslovakia in 1968. Czechoslovakia was already a communist, Soviet-aligned state, yet due to discord and internal division, the Soviets decided it was their business to forcibly intervene. This was part of the Brezhnev Doctrine (named after Soviet Premier Leonid Brezhnev), which stipulated that the Soviet Union could stage military interventions in fellow communist states if deemed necessary.

Considering the discord of the Cultural Revolution, Mao likely wondered if the Soviets were considering staging such an intervention in China. In consideration of all of this, Mao sought to distance himself from Soviet Russia and pull closer to the United States. Mao and Nixon shocked the world by forging a strong partnership with each other.

US President Richard Nixon meeting with Chairman Mao Zedong.[11]

Yes, China was communist, and America was capitalist, but these two found common ground with one another all the same. One major issue on Nixon's mind at this time was the Vietnam War. The war had been raging long before he became president and had been escalated primarily by his predecessor, President Lyndon Johnson. The war needed to come to an end, and Nixon wanted to be the president to conclude the conflict. Nixon and his advisers believed that China might hold the key to doing just that. The meeting had a lot on the table for the two to talk about, but the chance that China could weigh in and get the communist North Vietnamese to listen to reason was a big part of it. China was hoping to gain a bargaining chip against the Soviet Union, thereby increasing China's options and limiting dependence on the Soviets.

In 1972, shortly before Nixon's historic visit, Mao Zedong suffered a serious stroke that left him in declining health. Premier Zhou Enlai, already burdened with his own ailments, would be diagnosed two years later with terminal cancer. Both men knew their time was limited and began quietly considering who might carry the torch of leadership after them.

Both Mao and Zhou began pulling strings behind the scenes to try to bring their protégé, Deng Xiaoping, to prominence. This created a problem for Mao's wife, Jiang Qing, who was a big supporter of the Cultural Revolution. Her own radicals had previously denounced Deng during the purges for advocating certain economic reforms. They declared that he had deviated from Marxist doctrine. She and her most vocal supporters, who were later referred to as the Gang of Four, came out in direct opposition to Mao and Zhou's choice for a successor.

This created a schism in the Chinese government and society, leading to just the kind of power struggle that most people wanted to avoid. When the economy began to buckle and Chinese prosperity diminished, the winds began to shift back in favor of Deng. The Cultural Revolution was very unpopular by this point, as were Jiang and the Gang of Four. China was seemingly now ready to hear more of what Deng had to say.

In late 1975, as Zhou Enlai was stricken by illness, Deng Xiaoping was quietly elevated, taking charge of key state functions. But when Zhou died, the political tides turned sharply. The Gang of Four, which still wielded power, targeted Deng for his "capitalist deviations," and he was purged—just as his economic reforms were starting to gain traction. Only after Mao died and the radicals were swept aside did Deng's ideas finally begin to win out.

After Mao Zedong died at the age of eighty-two in 1976, the Chinese finally turned against Mao's wife Jiang and the Gang of Four. They were all put on trial. Jiang Qing was sentenced to death, although her sentence was commuted to life in prison. Her story ended in 1991 when she committed suicide. She hung herself in the hospital room where she was temporarily being treated for cancer. She left a sad suicide note in which she lamented the changes that were coming to China. One of the chief architects of the Cultural Revolution was apparently dismayed at what she viewed as a backtracking of the revolution. She spoke of how revisionists had ruined China and put an end to the revolutionary ideals she had helped champion. This might have been the end of her story, but it was also the end of a very tumultuous and frightening chapter of Chinese history.

Chapter 9: A Strange Mix of Repression and Reform

"One-sidedness means thinking in terms of absolutes, that is, a metaphysical approach to problems. In the appraisal of our work, it is one-sided to regard everything either as all positive or all negative. To regard everything as positive is to see only the good and not the bad, and to tolerate only praise and no criticism. To talk as though our work is good in every respect is at variance with the facts. It is not true that everything is good; there are still shortcomings and mistakes. But neither is it true that everything is bad, and that, too, is at variance with the facts."

-Mao Zedong[21]

In the aftermath of Mao Zedong's demise in 1976, there was a major shift in both China's overall political direction and those who were running the government. A figure little known outside China but already trusted in the upper ranks of the Communist Party emerged as Mao's successor. Hua Guofeng, who had once worked in public security and risen steadily through provincial posts in Hunan, had been handpicked by Mao for senior leadership. By the mid-1970s, he was serving as premier and first vice chairman of the Communist Party. He was hardly an outsider in Beijing politics, though he was still a surprise choice to many observers.

---

[21] Zedong, Mao. *Quotations from Chairman Mao Tse-Tung (The Little Red Book)*. Pg. 123.

In late 1978, more pragmatic heads prevailed. Under the leadership of Deng Xiaoping, China began charting a new course that deliberately distanced itself from Mao's most disastrous policies. Hua Guofeng's "Two Whatevers" line ("We will resolutely uphold whatever policy decisions Chairman Mao made, and unswervingly follow whatever instructions Chairman Mao gave") was quietly shelved, and the catastrophic Great Leap Forward was openly condemned. With Deng's emphasis on economic modernization and openness, the nation pivoted toward reforms that would shape China's trajectory for decades.

Correcting the disastrous agricultural policies of the Mao era proved to be a monumental task. It meant dismantling the communes and giving farmers more autonomy, paving the way for traditional farming and market-style exchanges in rural China. Instead of being forced to adhere strictly to government quotas (say, stocking eggs in bulk), farmers could now sell surplus produce freely, much like at a farmer's market. This return to localized markets and private enterprise, which was denounced by hardliners as dangerously capitalist, revived rural economies and brought family farms back to life.

This led to a great increase in agricultural profits that could be directly measured from 1979 to 1985. Farming improved, as did the environment. The 1970s saw the whole world begin to take a closer look at how human beings were affecting the environment. During this decade, for example, US President Richard Nixon established the Environmental Protection Agency (EPA).

By the end of the decade, the Chinese were starting to be better stewards as well. In sharp contrast to the days of killing sparrows, they had a much better grasp of the importance of sound environmental measures. This led to the passing of China's own Environmental Protection Law, which was focused on monitoring and enforcing environmental measures, in 1979.

By the time the 1970s came to a close and the 1980s dawned, China was back on the world stage in a big way. China had reestablished links with most major nations, even though it was still giving the cold shoulder to its former benefactor, the Soviet Union. Previous restraints on Chinese enterprise were slipping away, and new and exciting developments sprang up all over China. The gains made in the agricultural sector, in particular, allowed the Chinese government to mitigate many of the problems that had arisen in the urban sector.

However, in 1981, it became clear that the pace of investment needed to slow to prevent economic overheating. This did not sit well with old political hands who had championed massive industrial investment. They feared their benefits would be curtailed. The slowdown was temporary, though. By 1984, reforms were once again moving forward. Free enterprise was creating a competitive landscape in government and business, and price controls were being lifted in favor of market-based models.

Soon, new economic zones were being established in places like the Lower Yangtze, Fukien, and Kwangtung, where foreign investment was pouring in. In this new economic environment, bank loans suddenly took precedence over direct state funding. By 1985, even more reform measures were enacted, which brought even more benefits into the fields of both consumerism and industrial capacity.

Xiamen, one of the first special economic zones of China.[23]

Even so, since there was a decided lack of coordination, no standardization of the banking rules, and a bent toward inflation, some price controls had to be reintroduced in order to prevent long-term problems from erupting. This marked the return of some state controls on the Chinese economy.

As much as the Chinese experimented with a more liberal economy, the Chinese Communist Party remained relatively unchanged in its modus operandi. Unlike the Soviet Union, which was adopting its groundbreaking policy of glasnost (openness) and perestroika (restructuring) under Mikhail Gorbachev, the Chinese stuck to an authoritarian system that had little room for dissent or complaint.

The state of public affairs was decided to be wholly up to party officials and not something that could be democratically altered by the masses. This stronghold on Chinese society would prevent Chinese communism from totally collapsing. Unlike in Eastern Europe, there would be no toppling of Mao Zedong's statues in China.

Some scholars have argued that this sudden rush of economic liberalism after the crisis of the Cultural Revolution created a very strange situation in China. Suddenly, people were much better off, yet the communist leadership that had led them into the darkest of days was still in place.

Another interesting thing about China during this new period of openness was that many average Chinese citizens, for the first time ever, were getting a picture of how life in China compared to the rest of the world. Under Mao Zedong, the Chinese were faced with constant propaganda about how the capitalist countries of the world were evil and how the rest of the world's citizens were living in a state of slavery to greedy capitalists. The Chinese were now beginning to understand that much of the rest of the world was actually doing quite well and that their citizens were quite happy.

The Chinese began to look at their own country as it slowly rose from the economic and political wreckage of the past and realized just how far it lagged behind the developed world. This created a powerful desire to catch up, and there was a growing frustration with the slow pace of change among many young people. That frustration deepened in the spring of 1989 after the sudden death of reform-minded leader Hu Yaobang. His passing became the spark for massive demonstrations, which were led mostly by college students calling for political reform, greater freedoms, and an end to corruption. As weeks of peaceful protests unfolded in Beijing's Tiananmen Square, the world began to wonder if China might be on the brink of its own democratic breakthrough. But when the government sent in the army in early June, the result was a violent crackdown, forever cementing the events of 1989 as one of modern China's most infamous turning points.

The events of Tiananmen Square laid bare the chasm between China's intellectual elite and its ruling government. It seemed that this gap could not be bridged. Instead of dialogue, the state deployed troops, and the demonstrators were beaten—sometimes literally—into submission. In the aftermath, China's hardliners moved swiftly to roll back liberalization on every front.

This triggered a wave of international condemnation. The United States, Japan, and several European nations imposed sanctions, citing blatant human rights abuses. Yet, even within China's leadership, there was dissent. In 1992, Deng Xiaoping publicly broke with the hardliners, warning that their clampdowns had gone too far, particularly in reversing economic reforms that had begun to lift the country out of stagnation.

Deng's push to rein in the hardliners and revive economic reforms opened the door to a new chapter. The rest of the 1990s saw a steady return to relaxed controls, greater space for private enterprise, and, as a result, renewed prosperity. Southern China, in particular, experienced an economic boom, as private businesses flourished and fortunes were made almost overnight.

In his push to liberalize the economy of China, Deng often pointed to the example of Hong Kong. Hong Kong had been occupied by the British since the 19th century. The British would stick around until 1997, and even then, the economic and political system of their former colony was strikingly different than what was going on in China. Deng saw the economic prosperity in Hong Kong, and he used it as a model of how the rest of China should operate.

One of Deng's early supporters, Jiang Zemin, began to rise to prominence in the Chinese Communist Party. Jiang actually replaced high-profile Zhao Ziyang as general secretary in the immediate aftermath of the Tiananmen Square incident. He was also given the post of chairman of the Central Military Commission. Then, in 1993, he secured his place as president of the National People's Congress.

Deng had helped pave the way for Jiang to rise to power, and after Deng died in 1997, Jiang was able to further secure his grip, becoming China's paramount leader. Jiang presided over China during its momentous entry into the WTO (World Trade Organization) on December 11th, 2001. Interestingly, China became a member in the immediate aftermath of the World Trade Center attack in New York City, which took place on September 11th, 2001. Some historians have pointed out that it was during America's preoccupation with the 9/11 attacks and the subsequent war on terrorism that China truly rose to become a global power.

Chinese society was beginning to experience drastic changes due to one lingering holdover from Mao-style policies. Starting in 1979, China implemented its infamous one-child policy. This bit of social engineering was put in place to curb China's rapidly growing population and prevent a drain on resources. However, this policy led many Chinese families to try their hardest to have a son rather than a daughter. This was due to Chinese traditional thinking (which was never really eliminated by the Cultural Revolution) that a son was more preferable than a daughter. It was believed that boys took on a greater role as successors and, most importantly, as it pertained to their parents, in caring for the elderly.

Sadly, this led to many instances of aborted female babies so that families could produce that much-desired son. As the children of the one-child generation came of age in the 1990s, there was a noticeable imbalance between males and females. This, of course, would prove problematic when all of those sons found a very limited number of women available to marry.

Interestingly, another effect of the one-child policy was that for those who did choose to have a daughter and pinned all of the family hopes on that one child, there was a surge in empowerment and encouragement for these ambitious young women. The Communists always claimed to be champions of equality between males and females, and this new generation of females would put this proposed ideology to the test. Determined to do well and represent the interests of their families, Chinese universities were flooded with these young ladies who sought a good education and solid careers. As it turns out, even though most places in China might have had more boys than girls, Chinese colleges were perhaps the one place where girls were overrepresented.

Another effect of all of this was that a large number of girls who were not aborted ended up being given up for adoption. This was usually done by those who were still holding out for a male child. Parents did not register that they had a child with the state and then quietly dropped the baby off at the orphanage. As a result, orphanages swelled with all of these unwanted female babies.

Since the local Chinese were not likely to adopt them (that would defeat the whole purpose of seeking a male child), tremendous efforts were made to have these children adopted by parents from other countries, leading to large numbers of Chinese girls finding homes overseas. Demonstrating the reach of Maoist measures, the future of China had been significantly altered by this one policy alone.

Chapter 10: China During the 21st Century

"To be an official, you need to have the moral standing of an official—and that means not always thinking of yourself. A good cadre can be recognized by people no matter what their level is. Your constant thought needs to be, what can I do for the party? What will my legacy be?"

-Xi Jinping[22]

Deng's successor, Jiang Zemin, served as China's paramount leader from 1993 to 2003. He oversaw the British handover of Hong Kong in 1997, as well as the return of Macau from Portugal in 1999. He was the first Chinese leader to see the 21st century. He handed the reins of power over to his successor, Hu Jintao, who served from 2003 to 2013.

During Hu Jintao's regime, China gained more acceptance as an up-and-coming world power. Perception is everything, but hard, cold facts are pretty important too. No matter what anyone wanted to believe, China was making leaps and bounds as it pertained to its world standing. Financial statistics bear testament to this.

In 2007, China accounted for about 6 percent of the global gross domestic product—roughly one-sixteenth of the world's economy at the time. Since then, China's share has tripled to approximately 18 percent, firmly placing it second only to the United States.

---

[22] Brown, Kerry. *XI: A Study in Power*. 2022. Pg. 114.

One of China's crowning achievements during this period was hosting the 2008 Summer Olympics. Hu's time in office was known for its positive international trends, and it has been dubbed the *hexie* or "harmony" period by the Chinese. This was also due to the fact that Hu constantly referred to the need for a Socialist Harmonious Society. This was his answer to widening inequality and social unrest.

However, not everything was as harmonious as Hu and the government would have liked it to be. The very year China was stepping onto the world stage to host the 2008 Olympics, dramatic riots and protests took place in Tibet. Tibetans were wary of Chinese rule and sought to take advantage of international scrutiny over the Olympics to gain worldwide attention to their cause. There was widespread destruction of property during the unrest. Many people were injured, and some were even killed. The Chinese government pushed back hard against the rioters, and people were arrested in large numbers. The Chinese Communist Party also put a curfew in place to ensure that further unrest was quelled.

The crackdown in Tibet led to a larger police presence in Tibet's urban population centers. Much like an occupying army, armored units patrolled nonstop, making sure no one got out of line. They were not only on the lookout for protesters carrying signs or even rioters destroying property. They were also looking for Tibetan monks setting themselves on fire. As a form of ultimate protest, Tibetan monks were willing to set themselves ablaze in an act of self-immolation. The Chinese, ever conscious of their image, most certainly did not want the world to see such things play out on their television screens. China wished to present itself as a rising political and economic power. They had no room for Tibetan dissidents in their ambitious plans for the future.

The internet factored largely into China's renewed push for modernization. But almost immediately, the Chinese communist government faced the difficulty of trying to rein in or even censor what the average Chinese citizen was seeing on the internet. From unwanted news reports to pornographic material, Chinese officials were determined to monitor and, if necessary, censor what the Chinese had access to on the web.

This effort to safeguard the Chinese from objectionable (at least objectionable to the Chinese Communist Party) content would become known as the Great Firewall of China. Hot button topics such as the

Dalai Lama and the Tiananmen Square incident, for example, were blocked and kept firmly on the outside of this Great Firewall. The Great Firewall consisted of real-time human monitors who constantly examined materials being disseminated and software deployed on Chinese home computers that was designed to block questionable material. As of this writing, this system of censorship and surveillance is still in place.

Interestingly, in 2015, China's efforts to monitor its citizens online took a new turn. Alongside traditional internet censorship, new programs emerged that tracked and assessed certain aspects of people's behavior, particularly their financial reliability and legal compliance. While other countries have long relied on credit scores to measure one's ability to borrow money, China began piloting what became known as the Social Credit System. In practice, this was not a single, all-encompassing score but a patchwork of local government blacklists and private platforms, such as Alibaba's voluntary "Sesame Credit," that rewarded trustworthy conduct. The higher one's standing, the more conveniences and opportunities became available, from easier access to loans to waived deposits. Of course, the reverse could also be true for those who fell afoul of the rules, especially if they ignored court orders or failed to pay debts. The internet being what it is, one might imagine the system punishing people for disapproved hobbies, but these claims, such as fans of Japanese anime or video games being penalized, remain unsubstantiated.

This modern Social Credit System is not entirely new. It echoes an ancient Chinese tradition. During the medieval era, Daoist priests and later literati used ledgers of merit and demerit (*gongguoge*). These were papers or booklets in which people recorded daily good and bad deeds that were tabulated as moral points. Over the centuries, especially from the Song through the Qing dynasties, these ledgers became more widespread, not just as spiritual diaries but as frameworks for moral self-improvement and social guidance. Only now, with the technological infrastructure backed by state power, are comparable metrics being applied at scale but with vastly greater reach, impact, and enforcement.

In 2012, Hu Jintao's administration gave way to Chinese President Xi Jinping. Working from the same playbook as his predecessors, Xi Jinping came to prominence by becoming the head of his party, the head of the state, and the head of the army. This meant that he had political and governmental control, as well as solid military backing.

President Xi Jinping.[28]

President Xi's first few years were busy ones, as he embarked upon a wide range of initiatives. By 2018, Xi Jinping must have thought he still had plenty more left to do. That year, under his leadership, China's National People's Congress amended the constitution to remove the two-term limit for the presidency, opening the door for him to rule for as long as he chooses. Since then, Xi has wielded his authority with full force, consolidating power across the party, state, and military. He shows no signs of reversing course.

Under the ambitious rule of Xi Jinping, China embarked upon one of its greatest initiatives since Mao Zedong's Great Leap Forward. Dubbed the Belt and Road Initiative, this program sought to link China with other markets by creating infrastructure in foreign countries, such as roads and railways, to better distribute Chinese goods to places such as Africa, India, central Asia, and the Middle East.

The Great Leap Forward had focused on building up the infrastructure of China, but the Belt and Road Initiative turned outward. However, this was not just out of China's own kind-hearted beneficence. These road-building projects were created to bring China lucrative new markets in the places where the roads were being built. It also allowed for better transport of certain raw materials that China might want to ship along those roads and rail lines.

China, for example, has been widely criticized for its resource deals in Africa, especially in its pursuit of critical minerals such as cobalt and copper. These materials are essential for modern electronics and green technologies. These ventures often spark accusations of exploitation, with profits and benefits flowing disproportionately back to China. Yet, despite these motives, Beijing has also been praised for financing and building key infrastructure, from highways and railways to ports and power plants, bringing development to regions long overlooked by other global powers.

Even though the rest of the world might remain skeptical of the Chinese Communist Party's motives, Chinese officials wished to present China as a benign force for good on the world stage. Much like the United States was known for its efforts to aid struggling nation-states, China also wanted to create the appearance of a strong nation reaching down to help those who were less fortunate.

However, by the early 2020s, two big controversies would badly tarnish China's image. The first of these controversies centered on growing speculation over the fate of China's Uyghur Muslims. The Uyghurs are a Turkic people who have lived for centuries in China's far western Xinjiang region. While concerns about their treatment reached global headlines in the 2020s, reports describing the construction of sprawling "re-education" facilities stretch back to the 2010s. These centers, according to human rights groups, were aimed at erasing Uyghur customs and religious practices and replacing them with loyalty to the Chinese Communist Party.

In 2019, Chinese officials claimed many "trainees" had "graduated" and that some facilities had closed, but independent evidence suggested the network remained largely intact. To counter criticism, Beijing organized tightly controlled tours for diplomats and journalists, insisting its programs in Xinjiang were purely vocational and designed to combat extremism. Even so, new accusations in the 2020s again alleged widespread detention, mistreatment, and forced labor. China continues to reject these claims.

It was also in the early 2020s that the world was rocked by a global pandemic. While many aspects of the pandemic remain fiercely debated, the first major outbreak was detected in Wuhan, China, before spreading rapidly across the globe. The precise origin of the virus, whether from a natural spillover or another source, remains unproven. Still, critics have accused Chinese authorities of responding too slowly in the earliest days, allowing the outbreak to worsen. Considering how devastating the pandemic was to nations such as Iran, Russia, Britain, and the United States, some are surprised that the diplomatic blowback against Beijing has not been greater.

In theory, these nations could have united to condemn China or even demand some form of reparations. In practice, world leaders have largely settled for muted statements, while Chinese officials maintain they acted decisively. The WHO (World Health Organization) has echoed some of these assurances, though its own conduct during the pandemic drew heavy scrutiny and eroded public trust.

Even years later, the actions of both China and the WHO remain the subject of ongoing debate but not outright condemnation. While talk of holding China accountable surfaces from time to time, it remains firmly in the realm of speculation rather than action.

The general acceptance—grudging though it may be—of China's muted response to the global pandemic is perhaps one of the clearest signs of how far China's global standing has come. In the 19th and early 20th centuries, even a minor dispute involving China could provoke demands for immediate compensation. Under the Boxer Protocol, foreign powers wielded overwhelming leverage over Beijing.

Yet today, China could be the location of the first-known outbreak of a pandemic that crippled economies and disrupted lives across the planet, and it still faces no coordinated sanctions or demands for reparations. This change in attitude may have much to do with the powerful cards China holds—its political influence, its deep integration into global supply chains, and the economic dependencies it has cultivated with governments worldwide.

Iran offers a telling example. As a predominantly Muslim nation, one might expect it to voice concern over allegations of mass detention and repression of Uyghur Muslims in Xinjiang. Not long ago, Iran's supreme leader issued a fatwa (a legal ruling on Islamic law) against novelist Salman Rushdie for perceived insults to Islam. However, in the case of alleged abuses against Uyghurs, Tehran has remained silent. Deepening economic links with Beijing, along with possible strategic and military considerations, may explain this.

In fact, Iran was among the nations that sent parliamentary delegations to Xinjiang. The Iranian officials emerged from these tightly managed tours with public praise for China's "counter-terrorism" and "vocational training" programs. That endorsement is striking in light of history. Over a thousand years ago, during the Islamic conquest of Persia, parts of what is now Xinjiang saw waves of migrants and traders from Persian lands. This historical connection makes Tehran's unwillingness to support the Uyghurs today all the more remarkable.

Whether the Iranian delegations genuinely saw nothing amiss or simply chose not to acknowledge it, the outcome is the same. There were no follow-up investigations, no calls for accountability, and no break from Beijing's official narrative. Whatever is happening in Xinjiang remains behind a carefully maintained curtain, and Iran seems content to play its part in keeping it closed.

As you can see, China's ability to shape narratives now extends far beyond its borders. Corporations, athletes, and celebrities have all publicly backtracked after crossing Beijing's political red lines. China has long censored its own people, but the fact that its pressure can reach into the supposedly free press of other nations is remarkable.

Nevertheless, right or wrong, China and the Chinese Communist Party still stand strong. The Chinese Communist Party actually celebrated its 100th anniversary on July 1st, 2021. During an official event that was ostensibly meant to be a celebration, President Xi Jinping had some rather harsh and stark words for the rest of the world. He gave a speech in which he bluntly stated that any outside power attempting to interfere with China and Chinese policies would have their "heads bashed in."[23] His comment was apparently meant to be a vivid metaphor—an expression of China's growing resolve to defend its sovereignty and national interests in the face of foreign interference. Even so, it was clear to everyone listening that this was not the China of old and that it would not be pushed around.

China has a long history of being bullied and pushed around by outside powers. Whether it was the Mongols, the British, or the Japanese, foreign interference has left deep scars. In that light, it is understandable that Xi Jinping might frame his warnings to the outside world in sober, uncompromising terms. In earlier centuries, when China resisted invasions or foreign domination, its defiance was rooted in

---

[23] Brown, Kerry. *XI: A Study in Power*. Pg. 293.

genuine self-defense. However, future instances of what Beijing deems "interference" may not be so morally clear-cut.

Xi's language, for example, could just as easily be aimed at nations merely voicing concern over China's treatment of Uyghurs in Xinjiang. Beijing may dispute these allegations, but the notion that no one can even question Chinese actions pushes beyond defensive nationalism into an effort to shut down legitimate international scrutiny. Then there is the specter of Taiwan. If Chinese policy were to escalate to the bombing of Taiwan followed by a bloody invasion, Xi's warning would imply that outsiders should stand aside and let it happen, or risk, in his words, getting their "heads bashed" against a "Great Wall of steel."

It must be remembered that during his speech marking the Chinese Communist Party's 100th anniversary in July 2021, Xi was playing to a domestic audience full of senior party officials. Projecting toughness before such an audience was politically useful. Yet the entire world was also watching, and the force of his words rippled far beyond Tiananmen Square. That undercurrent still lingers as the international community watches with growing unease, waiting to see how this latest chapter in Chinese history will unfold.

Conclusion:
China—An Exercise in Strategic Patience

China is one of the oldest, continuous civilizations on the planet. Needless to say, it has gone through quite a few twists and turns in its history. China rose to prominence early on as the Middle Kingdom, with many satellite kingdoms surrounding it. Yet, even mighty China was ultimately overcome by the Mongol horde and made into just another piece of the Mongol khanate under the Yuan dynasty.

Although China was occupied by the Mongols, the undercurrent of Chinese civilization still survived. The Mongols remained impressed by China's Song dynasty—so much so that they sought to emulate it in their Yuan dynasty. The Mongols made use of Chinese inventions such as paper, rockets, gunpowder, and currency to shore up the strength of their own empire.

The Chinese spirit of innovation that brought about these great inventions was not going to abide Mongol occupation and usurpation forever. Eventually, the Chinese threw off their Mongolian yoke, which gave way to the majestic Ming dynasty. The Ming was arguably one of the greatest of all the Chinese dynasties.

Over time, the Ming dynasty weakened, and the Qing, whose leaders originated in Manchuria, overcame it. Some Ming loyalists went to Taiwan, where they tried to create their own alternative version of China. This state did not last, and soon the Qing controlled all of China and Taiwan.

It is striking to consider how often Taiwan has stood at a crossroads in China's destiny. The Ming loyalists once retreated here, holding out for two decades before the Qing took the island. Centuries later, the Qing themselves lost Taiwan to Japan. Then, in 1949, after years of brutal civil war, Chiang Kai-shek's Nationalists repeated history, retreating to Taiwan as the Communists consolidated power on the mainland.

Yet there is one major difference. Where the Ming lasted only a short while, the current government in Taiwan has endured for over seventy years, becoming an alternative Chinese state with its own identity and institutions. The Chinese Communist Party still insists Taiwan is an inalienable part of China, destined for "reunification," by force if necessary. That claim has kept the Taiwan question alive as one of the most enduring and dangerous issues in modern geopolitics.

If Beijing truly intends to seize Taiwan, and if Taiwan's allies, most notably the United States, are equally serious about its defense, the world could find itself staring at the fault line of a major war. Recent events show just how quickly such fault lines can rupture. Russia's invasion of Ukraine in 2022 and the renewed fighting between Israel and Hamas have both shaken the global order. A Taiwan conflict could be just as destabilizing—perhaps more so.

A war across the Taiwan Strait could draw in the US Navy, Japanese forces, and potentially South Korea. That, in turn, could tempt North Korea to side with Beijing and strike at its old enemies in the south. In 2024, North Korea and Russia signed a mutual aid treaty that was vague enough to leave Moscow wiggle room but concrete enough to raise the specter of Russian involvement in any East Asian war. If that happened, the world could face China, North Korea, and Russia as aligned combatants. With all three possessing nuclear weapons, with Russia having the largest arsenal in the world, the dangers would rise to existential levels.

And yet, perhaps it is precisely this idea of catastrophe that has so far stayed Beijing's hand. Chinese leaders know the risks as well as anyone. For now, they are practicing strategic patience, keeping the Taiwan question unresolved rather than igniting a war that could spiral beyond control. For the sake of China, Taiwan, and the rest of the world, one can only hope that patience endures.

Free limited time bonus

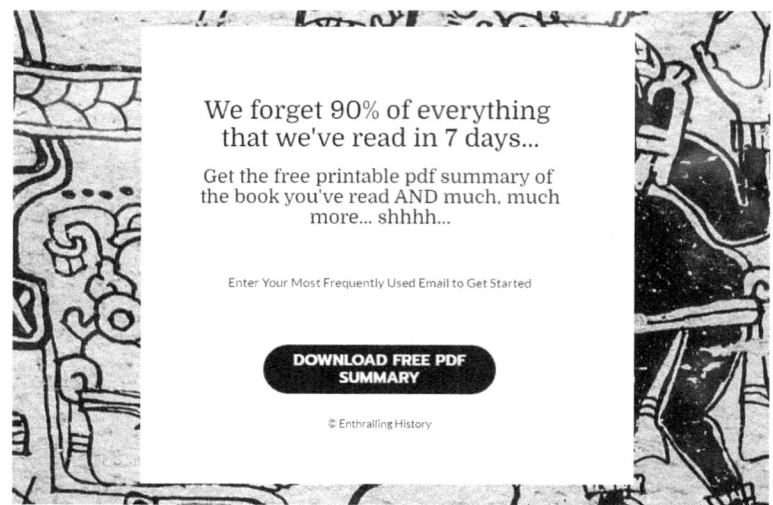

Stop for a moment. We have a free bonus set up for you. The problem is this: we forget 90% of everything that we read after 7 days. Crazy fact, right? Here's the solution: we've created a printable, 1-page pdf summary for this book that you're reading now. All you have to do to get your free pdf summary is to go to the following website:
https://livetolearn.lpages.co/enthrallinghistory/

Or, Scan the QR code!

Once you do, it will be intuitive. Enjoy, and thank you!

Here's another book by Enthralling History that you might like

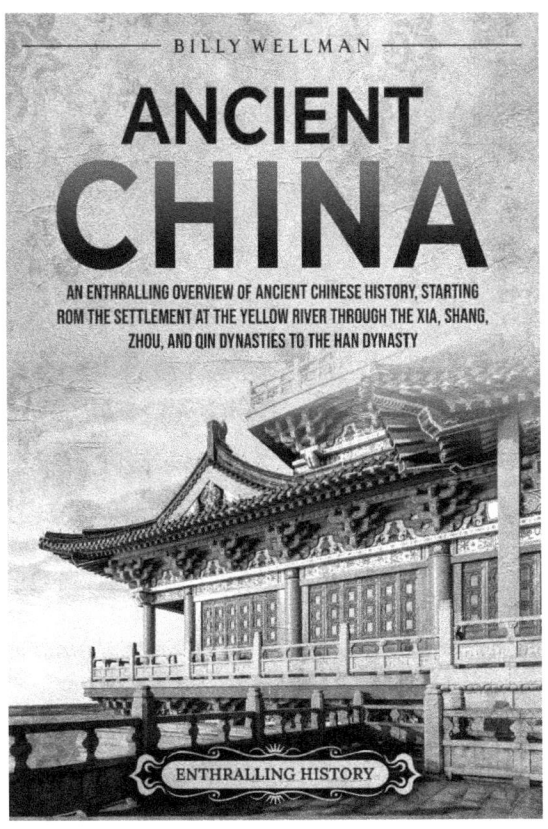

Further Reading and Reference

Benjamin, G. Craig. *The Big History of Civilizations.*

Brewer, D. *Quotes of Confucius and Their Interpretations: A Words of Wisdom Collection Book.* 2020.

Brown, Kerry. *XI: A Study in Power.* 2022.

Clements, Jonathan. *A Brief History of China.* 2019.

Gernet, Jacques. *A History of Chinese Civilization.* 1972.

Gray, Henry John. *China: A History of the Laws, Manners and Customs of the People.* 1878.

Keay, John. *China: A History.* 2008.

Min, Anchee. *China: People, Place, Culture, History.* 2007.

Pletcher, Kenneth. *The History of China.* 2010.

Stuart-Fox, Martin. *A Short History of China and Southeast Asia: Tribute, Trade, and Influence.* 2003.

Tanner, Harold. *China: A History From the Great Qing Empire through the People's Republic of China, 1644-2009.* 2010.

Zedong, Mao. *Quotations from Chairman Mao Tse-Tung (The Little Red Book).* Pg. 1964.

Image Sources

1 SSYoung, CC BY-SA 4.0 <https://creativecommons.org/licenses/by-sa/4.0>, via Wikimedia Commons, https://commons.wikimedia.org/wiki/File:Teeth_of_Yuanmou_Man_(Cast)_-_cropped.png

2 Siyuwj, CC BY-SA 4.0 <https://creativecommons.org/licenses/by-sa/4.0>, via Wikimedia Commons, https://commons.wikimedia.org/wiki/File:Distant_dialogue_exhibition_of_Dadiwan_site,_2017-03-04_05.jpg

3 Daderot, CC0, via Wikimedia Commons, https://commons.wikimedia.org/wiki/File:Turquoise-Inlaid_Plaque_with_Stylized_Animal-Mask_Decoration,_1900-1350_BC,_Neolithic_to_Shang_period,_Erlitou_culture,_China,_bronze_with_turquoise_inlay_-_Sackler_Museum_-_DSC02627.JPG

4 Mlogic, CC BY-SA 3.0 <https://creativecommons.org/licenses/by-sa/3.0>, via Wikimedia Commons, https://commons.wikimedia.org/wiki/File:HouMuWuDingFullView.jpg

5 Territories_of_Dynasties_in_China.gif: Ian Kiu, CC BY-SA 3.0 <http://creativecommons.org/licenses/by-sa/3.0/>, via Wikimedia Commons, https://commons.wikimedia.org/wiki/File:Zhou_dynasty_1000_BC.png

6 Philg88, CC BY-SA 3.0 <https://creativecommons.org/licenses/by-sa/3.0>, via Wikimedia Commons, https://commons.wikimedia.org/wiki/File:EN-WarringStatesAll260BCE.jpg

7 SY, CC BY-SA 4.0 <https://creativecommons.org/licenses/by-sa/4.0>, via Wikimedia Commons, https://commons.wikimedia.org/wiki/File:Han_Expansion.png

8 Ian Kiu, CC BY-SA 3.0 <https://creativecommons.org/licenses/by-sa/3.0>, via Wikimedia Commons, https://commons.wikimedia.org/wiki/File:Western_Jeun_Dynasty_280_CE.png

9 Charlie fong, CC BY-SA 4.0 <https://creativecommons.org/licenses/by-sa/4.0>, via Wikimedia Commons, https://commons.wikimedia.org/wiki/File:Hangingtemple20190929.jpg

10 Yug, CC BY-SA 3.0 <https://creativecommons.org/licenses/by-sa/3.0>, via Wikimedia Commons, https://commons.wikimedia.org/wiki/File:China,_742.svg

11 SS, CC BY-SA 4.0 <https://creativecommons.org/licenses/by-sa/4.0>, via Wikimedia Commons, https://commons.wikimedia.org/wiki/File:Later_Han.png

12 https://commons.wikimedia.org/wiki/File:Leifeng_Pagoda_in_the_Southern_Song_Dynasty_by_Li_Song.jpg

13 Cattette, CC BY 4.0 <https://creativecommons.org/licenses/by/4.0>, via Wikimedia Commons, https://commons.wikimedia.org/wiki/File:Yuan_Dynasty_revised.png

14 https://commons.wikimedia.org/wiki/File:A_Seated_Portrait_of_Ming_Emperor_Taizu.jpg

15 Philg88: Attribution Wikimedia Foundation, www.wikimedia.org, CC BY 4.0 <https://creativecommons.org/licenses/by/4.0>, via Wikimedia Commons, https://commons.wikimedia.org/wiki/File:Qing_Empire_circa_1820_EN.svg

16 shizhao, CC BY-SA 2.0 <https://creativecommons.org/licenses/by-sa/2.0>, via Wikimedia Commons, https://commons.wikimedia.org/wiki/File:%E9%A2%90%E5%92%8C%E5%9B%AD%E4%B8%87%E5%AF%BF%E5%B1%B1%E4%BD%9B%E9%A6%99%E9%98%81.jpg

17 https://commons.wikimedia.org/wiki/File:Regaining_the_Provincial_Capital_of_Ruizhou.jpg

18 https://commons.wikimedia.org/wiki/File:Sunyatsen1.jpg

19 https://commons.wikimedia.org/wiki/File:Yuan_Shikai2.jpg

20 https://commons.wikimedia.org/wiki/File:Chinese_captives_in_Nanking.jpg

21 https://commons.wikimedia.org/wiki/File:President_Richard_Nixon_and_Mao_Zedong.jpg

22 周流劲火, CC BY 2.5 <https://creativecommons.org/licenses/by/2.5>, via Wikimedia Commons, https://commons.wikimedia.org/wiki/File:Xiamen_Shimao_Straits_Tower_at_dusk.jpg

23 Officia do Palácio do Planalto, CC BY 2.0 <https://creativecommons.org/licenses/by/2.0>, via Wikimedia Commons, https://commons.wikimedia.org/wiki/File:Xi_Jinping_2019.jpg